THE *Changing* ENVIRONMENT OF LIBRARIES

THE *Changing* ENVIRONMENT OF LIBRARIES

Papers delivered at the
1970–71 Colloquium Series,
Graduate School of Librarianship,
University of Denver

Edited by

JOHN T. EASTLICK

American Library Association
Chicago 1971

International Standard Book Number 0–8389–0113–1 (1971)
Library of Congress Catalog Card Number 79–176325
Copyright © 1971 by the American Library Association

All rights reserved. No part of this publication may be reproduced in any form without permission in writing from the publisher, except by a reviewer who may quote brief passages in a review.

Printed in the United States of America

Contents

	Acknowledgments	vii
John T. Eastlick	*Introduction*	1
Ralph W. Conant	THE *Sociological* ENVIRONMENT	4
Frank S. Mathews	THE *Technological* ENVIRONMENT	20
Ralph E. Ellsworth	THE *Institutional* ENVIRONMENT	30
David H. Clift	THE *Organizational* ENVIRONMENT	39
Lloid B. Jones	THE *Educational* ENVIRONMENT	60
John T. Eastlick	THE *Librarian's* ENVIRONMENT	73

Acknowledgments

I wish to thank and pay tribute to the speakers who participated in the 1970–71 Colloquium Series at the University of Denver. Not only were they willing to participate, but they freely gave the Graduate School of Librarianship permission to publish their papers with the understanding that any monetary return from publication would be utilized to provide scholarships for worthy students—worthy students regardless of race or creed.

I also wish to thank Mrs. Sally Proesel and Miss Leah Rae Miron for their assistance in typing and proofreading. Without the teamwork of the faculty and staff of the Graduate School of Librarianship this publication would not have been possible.

JOHN T. EASTLICK

Introduction

Every profession should have its philosophers—individuals who can observe the vast panorama of world events and synthesize the stresses and strains, the new and the obsolete, the wise and the foolish into recognizable patterns. To do such prediction or forecasting is, of course, a dangerous activity. It can be valid only to the degree that the philosopher is wise and the reader is willing to examine but evaluatively challenge such predictions.

Unfortunately the emerging library profession has no philosophers. We tend to drift along with the existing social, economic, and cultural stream. What is even worse, we tend to drift not at the fore of this stream where there is rushing, bursting activity, but in the quieter backwater—always following and never leading. Perhaps it is the nature of an institution like a library to move cautiously, to maintain carefully the recorded knowledge of man's past activities, achievements, and foibles. Perhaps the historical role of libraries which causes the institution to look backward still dominates the thinking of the majority of people who direct library activities.

But the historical role of libraries, the importance of which will not be challenged, is not enough to meet today's problems. Certainly it is inadequate to meet tomorrow's needs. We casually say that change comes slowly, and this has been true, with few exceptions, throughout history. Granted the Renaissance, the Industrial Revolution, and the European wars of the 1840s were periods of dramatic intellectual expansion, cultural development, and social change. But with those exceptions man has tended to drift comfortably in his security of well-established life-styles.

Then came Sputnik I. A shock spread throughout America which reverberated in our classrooms, our institutions, and our government.

Change accelerated in the United States, and demands for change spread throughout the entire world—certainly to those nations not rigidly controlled and regimented. In those nations where people had the freedom to express their own opinion, previous concepts of governmental responsibility, institutional reliability, religious authority, family integrity, and individual behavior were challenged or changed.

All types of libraries have been affected by the changes which have occurred. The technological revolution, the knowledge and population explosion, the increasing threat to our environment, the shrinking of world boundaries due to advances in rapid transportation and communication, the mobility of our population, and the changing occupational pattern of our citizens all have had an immediate impact on libraries. Libraries as traditional institutions have found it difficult to cast off their bureaucratic structure and to develop new avenues of effectiveness to meet the problems of racial and minority unrest, student demonstrations, the generation gap, citizens who are unemployed because of job displacement, higher crime rates, and skyrocketing inflation.

The problems which are with us today are not going to go away or become less vital to society. Many are going to become more dominant and pressing. To solve these existing problems, or even to offer partial solutions, changes in our present societal structures will have to be made. These changes will tear at the basic fabric of which American culture is made. But what of the changes yet to come? Science—the chemist, the biologist, and the doctor—already has developed the capability of performing miracles: the organ transplant, the creation of life in a test tube, the modification of genes, the creation of man to man's desire. The increased mobility of man in his job and social environment is challenging family relationships, his identification with the community, his interpersonal associations with people, his participation in those religious and charitable institutions which enrich and stabilize an individual.

The rapidity of change in the next ten years will challenge the sanity of man. To keep up, to be informed, and to adapt to these changes while maintaining mental stability is the coming crucible of America.

Believing that a library has a great contribution to make, not only to those who are causing change but also to those who must understand change, we at the Graduate School of Librarianship, University of Denver, have tried to look ahead to see what the library environment will be in the future. We believe that only if we understand where we are going can we guide libraries into viable, relevant roles. For this reason the Graduate School of Librarianship, in planning its

1970–71 Colloquium Series, decided to focus attention on changes which are occurring in various segments of our society and their effect on libraries. Naturally not all the social problems and issues facing libraries could be explored during one academic year. Rather, it was our purpose to select certain areas which seemed of primary concern to libraries and to have those subjects discussed by qualified people.

A Colloquium Series of the Graduate School of Librarianship at the University of Denver is presented each academic year to provide students the opportunity to hear and to discuss current library trends and problems with prominent librarians or individuals whose expertise influences libraries. In addition to students of the Graduate School of Librarianship, practicing librarians from the Rocky Mountain region and interested members of the public attend and participate. Five Colloquium lectures were presented between January and May 1971. The papers of these lectures are presented as the first five chapters of this book. The last chapter has been added in order to cover another major area in which change is occurring—that of the library.

After each of the Colloquium lectures, a seminar was held during which time students, faculty, and guests could question the speaker and the speaker had an opportunity to expand on his basic paper. It is regretted that the seminar discussions were not taped and reported herein, as many valuable insights into the future library environment were gained from them.

RALPH W. CONANT

THE *Sociological* ENVIRONMENT

We Americans are embarked on an era of extraordinary change rooted in new and rapidly developing knowledge about our physical and social environment. We have learned how to curtail most diseases afflicting the human body, and we are on the verge of perpetuating man's life-span far beyond the seventh decade. We know how to control environmental threats to human life, and we are gradually converting this knowledge into effective political and administrative mechanisms. In a little more than a decade of effort, we have produced the technical capability for exploring other planets.

Knowledge feeds upon knowledge, and its growth in our age is assured by an educated constituency eager for the excitement of new discovery. The expansion of knowledge is encouraged by the ready patronage of political leaders who see the products of scientific inquiry as new sources of power. Man's capacity to anticipate and solve physical problems does not necessarily transfer to social and political problems, yet the search for solutions to these most critical problems now constitutes a major intellectual and physical effort. Moreover, the concentration on solutions to the problems of war, poverty, and disordered behavior will continue to increase. The present trend among college youth toward the social sciences and the humanities is evidence.

Social innovation is going through a period of trial-and-error inventiveness that characterized technological innovation at a comparable

Dr. Conant is professor of political science and director of the Institute of Urban Affairs at the University of Houston. An expert on violence and regional planning, he edited *The Public Library and the City* (Cambridge, Mass.: MIT Press, 1965) and has written numerous articles concerning the impact of urbanization on libraries. The original draft of this manuscript was entitled "The Future of Libraries."

stage. Confronted with enormous costs and spasmodic payoffs, political leaders who must have political profit out of social experimentation will eventually change the present hit-and-miss strategy of social problem-solving to highly rational methods. What are needed, of course, are new tools of social analysis which will provide policymakers with a systematic understanding of the social problems for which they are seeking solutions.

I believe we have entered an era in which man's intellect—his ideas, aspirations, plans, and problem-solving capacity—will hold sway. This is already true in problem areas susceptible to the physical sciences, and we are moving toward the intellectual attack in social and political areas. This means that our intellectual institutions—universities, libraries, and research industries—are moving into positions of central influence in determining the course of man's activities.

Those institutions that move with change and maintain a position of relevance to contemporary problems will fulfill themselves. Others will simply wither and be absorbed by the more vigorous and imaginative ones. Libraries will fare according to their individual quality and leadership. Those that are part of a larger institution will, of course, have little choice in their destiny except to be technically competent and farsighted in terms of institutional objectives. Independent libraries will keep ahead of fast-moving intellectual activity only if they are in close touch with major trends of the times and adapt services to them. The trends that yield the most useful clues to change are: (1) population growth and distribution in urban areas, (2) expanding knowledge, (3) technological advances, (4) increasing wealth and declining poverty, and (5) evolving governmental policies requiring intergovernmental cooperation and interinstitutional planning.

Population Trends

The population of the United States may reach 350,000,000 by the year 2000 when, according to some experts, it is likely to reach a permanent plateau of growth. While many demographers are still predicting a doubling of population every thirty-five years beyond the turn of the century, present trends belie this pessimistic outlook. Whereas birth rates climbed steadily from 1935 to 1957, they have been receding ever since. From an all-time high of 26 live births per thousand in 1957, the rate had fallen below 17 per thousand by 1969—the lowest ever recorded. The availability and widening acceptance of new types of contraceptives plus extensive private and public efforts to promote education and research in population control are paying off. This gradual leveling will be noticeable by 1985.

Population statistics for the United States as a whole are of limited value to librarians whose institutions are located in areas where population trends are far out of line with national averages. Birth rates among blacks in central-city ghettos are much higher than among whites in other areas. Migration patterns within and between cities are locally unique and fluctuate over time. The migration patterns of cities, of course, have a much greater impact on individual library markets than simple population growth has. It is apparent, for example, that northern and western cities whose nonwhite populations were still below 30 percent in 1970 will experience massive shifts within the next decade or two of the character experienced by cities whose nonwhite populations were over 40 percent in 1970. As the blacks and browns move in, the whites disperse. It was evident by 1960, and even more so by 1970, that central-city populations were thinning out and dispersing to suburbs. Thus central cities, especially in the North and the West, cannot yet foresee the time when their presently fluctuating populations will stabilize. Eventually, however, conditions in central cities will be so improved that a sizable middle-class population will be lured back. A back-to-the-city trend began to be strongly evident in the early 1960s among affluent young singles, the older middle class whose children had grown up, and the well-to-do who could afford to send their children to private schools.

The Intellectual Revolution

In spite of significant gaps in opportunities for education, we Americans have firmly established the principle of public responsibility for quality education through vocational, graduate, or professional schools. Equality of educational opportunities is still severely restricted in nonwhite and poverty sections of cities and in rural and underdeveloped areas. Only a few states have undertaken a full range of higher education facilities at nominal direct cost to students. Teacher education is still a long way from the standard of excellence set by a few outstanding graduate schools of education. Yet the states are on the move, and the federal government is allocating increasing resources to education at all levels. In a decade or so no local school system will want for the support to provide an acceptable education for all youth. In a few years no qualified student will lack for an opportunity to attend a college or university. No youth who wants technical skills or ordinary job training will be denied an appropriate opportunity. The federal Manpower Act of 1962 laid the groundwork for such training programs; the new Manpower Act of 1970 continued and broadened established programs.

Thus, by 1985, our public educational system will be fully structured and adequately financed, and the variety of training offered will come close to meeting all the requirements of our postindustrial society, in which more than one-half of the employed population is involved in an occupation other than the production of food, clothing, shelter, and other necessary goods. The apparent turning point came in 1956, the year white-collar workers first outnumbered the blue-collar workers. Actually, the transition has been rapid ever since 1940 when the nation geared its industrial capacity to meet the demands of the Second World War. In that pivotal year there were 3.9 million professional and technical workers, making up 7.9 percent of the labor force; by 1975 there will be an estimated 12.4 million, making up 14.2 percent of the labor force.

Expanding educational opportunities coupled with an expanding demand for highly trained workers, both professional and subprofessional, indicate a corresponding demand for sophisticated educational experiences provided by institutions responsible for formal training. Libraries, commercial distributors of educational materials, cultural organizations, schools, and universities will have continuing demands upon them to keep skills in tune with the rush of new knowledge and new techniques. The special role of libraries is to provide the materials of continuing education that are not available from any other source in the community. If the public library is to assume primary responsibility in this area (as it should), it must develop methods to identify the needs in the community and take steps to meet them.

New Technologies

The application of radical new technologies in older cities of the United States will be slow, especially in the fields of housing and mass transportation. We have too much investment in old techniques, old habits, and old hardware to move quickly to new modes. Yet the demands for improvements in housing, transportation, communications, waste disposal, water supply, and other key facilities are pressing hard on policy leaders. The demands to make cities more comfortable, convenient, and economical will eventually prevail, but only gradually.

Improved urban transportation will create market areas for public and private institutions in cities several times greater than present ones. Moreover, the coverage, convenience, and economy of new modes of urban transportation will permit libraries and other cultural institutions a wide choice of locations within the urban region. In many cases, it will be feasible to place specialized segments of such institutions in locations serving a specialized clientele. New applications of communications coupled with information storage and retrieval techniques will further the feasibility of scattered locations in response to market demands.

Improved multiple-housing design in central cities will be a critical factor in attracting the affluent middle class back into the city. Large condominiums with built-in community facilities, and perhaps built-in schools, might be the answer. Large tracts of "urban renewal" land in central cities will be available to meet the inevitable upsurge in the family housing market anticipated around 1973—the year the "war babies" will begin moving into the housing market in great numbers. By then the inflation crisis which drove interest rates to astronomical levels and crimped the housing market in 1969 and 1970 will have subsided.

If imaginative and practical-minded designers succeed in bringing to the heart of cities moderately priced, aesthetically planned residential units that "feel" more like a house than an apartment, a revolution could occur in the present preference for suburbs over central city. The flight from the city was, after all, a flight from the tenement, from lifestyles associated with poverty, and from lower-status newcomers. At the present time there is still no widely available and acceptable alternative within the central areas of cities for middle-income families. Schools are a problem, but they would not be if there were enough middle-class children in cities to populate them.

The technological revolution will place new kinds of demands on libraries and other institutions in the knowledge industry, but at the same time will offer opportunities for adapting old institutions to new requirements and new opportunities.

The End of Economic Poverty

Within a decade or so the poor among us will be those who are dependent on society because of physical or psychological incapacity. Even these individuals will have minimum resources for the necessities of life, for everyone in the nation whose income falls below a defined poverty line will benefit from a flexible income-maintenance program sponsored by the federal government. The Nixon administration's welfare program in which all families receive a minimum income is the beginning. The beneficiaries of this program will, by and large, use the subsidy as a basis of family and personal stability and as a foundation on which to build toward economic self-sufficiency. The income supplement program and the purposes to which most beneficiaries will put it will bring into the knowledge-industry market a whole new segment of the population, whose previous educational level and state of demoralization were so great that many of them could not relate in any effective way to educational and training opportunities ostensibly open to them.

Education will be among the priority demands of families emerging from poverty, as it has been in the past. When the poor emerge from poverty via the guaranteed income supplement, they will turn first to public institutions for guidance toward opportunity. In this context Dan Lacy urges that libraries assume active responsibility for expressing demand and providing channels of distribution for materials needed by segments of society not effectively literate; that is to say, the public library has an additional responsibility in the adult education field to identify and make available materials which can increase effectiveness of the educationally disadvantaged in the community. Lacy explains that private publishers are effectively confined to the middle- and upper-class segments of society because their purchasing power is adequate to sustain the publishers' machinery of distribution.

Edward Banfield's pessimistic view of the library's capacity to serve the poor is qualified in the following passage:

> If one believes that lower-class adults can be enticed to read, there is much to be said for making this the primary purpose of the library and for trying any approach that offers the least promise.[1]

Libraries, of course, cannot and should not try to take on an educational task, except in the traditionally passive sense. But once the poor are helped out of destitution and hopelessness, the incentive to move to a self-sustaining economic level will be very great among most of them. Libraries and other public institutions of the inner city, where the poor will continue to live for a long time hence, must be prepared to contribute to the dignity and self-education of the poverty residents.

INSTITUTIONAL CENTRALIZATION AND PLANNING

The long-standing trend toward large-scale enterprises, both public and private, is a correlate of population growth, concentration in cities, specialization in the labor force, an expanding economy, and an ever rising standard of living. These factors add up to bigness in almost all forms of organized human activity. The bigger and wealthier we become, the more knowledge we acquire, the better technologies we produce, the more incentive we have to convert these advantages to profit via the scale economies of large organizations. But once the pay-offs of centralization are realized and the wealth accumulated, we may then reverse the process of centralization to personalize services through concurrent decentralization while maintaining the beneficial features of large-scale operations.

With respect to libraries, the outpouring of new book titles in nonfiction categories compels new space, larger staffs, a more efficient division of labor, and improved intellectual and technical skills within each individual library institution. By the year 2000, when present staff recruits will be directors and department heads, the demand for library services will have risen severalfold. Present libraries will not necessarily be larger, for competing institutions may take over some library services; and staffs may not increase greatly, for machines will do routine operations such as book selection, cataloging, and repetitive reference. Even individual library buildings may not need to be much larger, for library institutions will probably occupy several locations. Nevertheless, the services that libraries now monopolize will expand, not in direct proportion to the rise in population, but with the rise in educational levels, the accelerating pace of technological development, and the shift to predominance in scientific problem-solving.

If the library profession is to hold its customary place among the major facilities that meet the intellectual demands of the future, library administrators must acquire sophisticated new skills in institutional management and make plans for a new scale and style of institutional development. A matter of immediate priority is the establishment of network libraries in metropolitan areas. These networks in most places must cross municipal boundary lines, which almost everywhere are hard to breach unless required by some higher authority at the state or federal level.

Perhaps the most serious obstacle to effective network libraries will be the need to create hierarchies of libraries and specialized facilities within the networks so that they serve the widest possible range of clientele. The trouble comes when some library units within systems are seen by librarians as more prestigious, more challenging, and more interesting than others. As long as existing municipal boundary lines give public library administrators the option of autonomy, they are likely to prefer the independence to participation in a metropolitanwide system.

Nevertheless, centralized regional library institutions and a carefully planned hierarchical network of subregional library facilities could assure a key role for public libraries in the next half century. Studies of present institutions and the tentative linkages among them by systems analysis and cost-benefit analyses already support this conclusion. Actually, library administrators and municipal officials will not have very much choice in the matter. For some years the federal government has been constructing a policy of intergovernmental and metropolitan planning and cooperation. Title II of the 1966 Demonstration Cities and Metropolitan Development Act includes libraries in the requirement of a metropolitan planning review of applications for certain federal loans and grants. The review must be made by a regional planning agency which also reviews grant applications for most other federally sponsored projects in the urban region.

Even though there are still no specific requirements for metropolitan library networks in present federal legislation or administrative policy, it would be shortsighted of library leaders to put off action, for the complexities of life in metropolitan communities together with the inadequacies of local government are forcing the state and federal governments to take major responsibility for planning the physical and social development of cities. The broadening role of the state and federal governments has encouraged and supported the multipurpose regional planning agencies. These agencies are now operating in the Standard Metropolitan Statistical Areas (SMSA) throughout the country and form the skeletal structure of a system of future de facto metropolitan governments.

When they are fully developed, these agencies will be the means by which local communities will be rid of services such as comprehensive public and research libraries requiring a regional organizational base to administer. These agencies will also be the apparatus through which federal and state governments may decentralize programs requiring local and regional direction. This network of metropolitan planning agencies will permit a more equitable distribution of government services and resources from all levels of government than we have ever had before.

Two Societies

One cannot write about the problems of American cities without including a discussion of the consequences of the ghettoization of blacks, Mexican-Americans, and other excluded minorities. One can no longer discuss the political and social aspects of institutional change in the central city without primary reference to the twin phenomena of white dispersion and black confinement. One cannot discuss serving the unserved in our central cities without focusing on ghetto communities and their complex requirements, because the central city of the next three or four decades will be black (and brown) in its voting majority, its politics and political decision-making apparatus, the fabric of neighborhood society, and the clientele of its public institutions.

Our central cities have already become isolated walled-off ghettos of uniformly restricted opportunity. The physical ghetto has created a psychological ghetto characterized by fear, suspicion, antagonism, frustration, misunderstanding, and mutual ignorance of life-styles and aspirational values. The psychological ghetto is itself a barrier to opportunity and mainstream acculturation. The psychological ghetto is imposed and reinforced by the dominant white community, but its conditions are absorbed and internalized by the minority community it affects. It shows up in the reluctance of blacks to participate in the white community even when opportunities are open. Witness the slowness of middle-class blacks to move into predominantly white neighborhoods that *are* open, of black parents to have their children bussed to white schools, and the preference of blacks and other minorities for neighborhood services even when downtown merchants solicit their business. The fear of a painful and degrading confrontation with hostile or condescending whites is justified by contact with some whites whose conscious or unconscious attitudes and actions are what minorities call "racist."

The psychological ghettoization is the consequence of a pervasive (often unintentional) attitude of paternalism on the part of whites. Some examples are: going out of one's way to be helpful or kind to blacks because they are black (the attitude of some white welfare workers); the suppressed hostility (becoming angry at nonappreciative blacks because one is trying so hard); active resentment toward a black who violates some persisting taboo (dating or marrying a white); price and rent discrimination on some spurious excuse (a high rate of pilferage); differential police behavior between white and black communities.

Many of the largest cities in America will eventually be run by blacks and other minorities when their numbers become predominant in those cities. I have estimated that a dozen or so major cities will have black mayors and black bureaucracies by 1985 or sooner. This will occur because the myopic white majority has wished it to be so. Even if they decided otherwise tomorrow, the trend in central cities is irreversible. Even if our national open-housing policies were invoked as local policy in 1970, it would take two generations of suburban-bound blacks to achieve a dispersal comparable to that of whites.

The white institutions of the central city (prominent among which are public libraries) that serve central-city clientele must adopt new organizational behavior patterns and staffing modes. They must have the staff who know, or learn to appreciate and respect, the values and aspirations of clientele in the community they serve. The typical black urban community is extraordinarily diverse and complex, far more so than the typical white urban or suburban community, because blacks of all economic and social levels live in the black communities of cities. They cannot disperse, as whites can, into homogeneous communities throughout the metropolis. Thus, serving the heterogeneous black communities of central cities cannot be according to the traditional norms, habits, values, and objectives of white librarians in white communities.

Central-city institutions which come within the purview and influence of local government will eventually be shaped by political leaders as the majority of voters want them to be. The unserved of the present day will be served as they wish to be served within a few years after their voting strength produces officeholders from their own ranks.

As black leaders take over the political apparatus of central cities, they may temporarily insist upon the focus of local institutions inward. Black mayors, black librarian administrators, and black voters will be less interested in the participation of city-supported libraries in a metropolitan library system than are the present white administrators of central-city libraries. Black political leaders are likely to condone a metropolitan orientation only insofar as they cannot prevent it or it serves an inner-city purpose.

FUNCTIONS OF LIBRARIES IN THE FUTURE

It seems to me that libraries of all types should continue to be what they have traditionally been—facilities for the collection and dissemination of cultural and educational materials within the communities they serve. But library leaders face the problem of defining what materials fall within the cultural and educational categories in terms of the market of individual library institutions. What may be frivolous for the users of a research library might be appropriate for users of an urban public library in a culturally deprived neighborhood.

Library leaders themselves must define the various markets of different kinds of library institutions as an aid in distinguishing appropriate goals from inappropriate ones. Most public libraries know their current clientele, but few know the nature of their *potential* market in terms of additional services people might want if such were made available. Library leaders face the problem of adapting the organization and management of individual institutions to the changing requirements of shifting markets and to new modes of storing and presenting materials. Finally, library leaders face the problem of striking a balance between centralized and decentralized organization within library institutions and establishing interinstitutional arrangements in a workable hierarchy of specializations that achieve a full range of library services in and among metropolitan communities.

As matters now stand, the public libraries of suburban communities may become a little larger and a little more sophisticated in the decades ahead; but they are not destined to compete in services with research libraries, with the bulk of demand in fiction reading, or with the specialty reference requirements of modern industry. If school libraries catch on, the public library may be relieved of a very large proportion of its student clientele. What then will be left for the small suburban library? A margin of the fiction market, household and family reference services, circulation of musical records, and preschool reading services. A few suburban libraries will offer facilities for community activities such as reading and discussion groups, lectures, and documentary and special-interest films.

An evolving function of suburban libraries will be as a local outlet in a regional system. The role of the suburban library in the metropolitan network will depend on several factors: what other kinds of library facilities are in the system; what kinds of materials are available from the system; how research and special libraries choose to serve their clientele; whether any significant portion of these demands can be met through local distribution points in suburban branches; and, from the standpoint of the consumer, whether local public libraries are logistically the most convenient and efficient pickup point for such materials.

Public libraries in the big central cities have literally grown up with those cities, catering primarily to the needs of the middle class and to the striving lower classes. These libraries have been an oasis of learning for the self-taught, a research resource for students, a sanctuary for loners, a depository for an endless variety of published and unpublished materials. In recent times, the big city public library has endeavored to be a neighborhood reading room and distribution point by providing branch locations in areas where the demand for services seemed to warrant the effort.

A few of the larger, better endowed libraries have become cultural and research centers of high standing. These institutions harbor collections that are the envy of some of the young giants among the state universities whose own research collections fall far short of the requirements for graduate programs.

What is the future of the big city libraries? Actually, there is no one developmental trend likely to be predominant in the period ahead. Development in the past rode the wave of demand for a diversified but accessible cultural resource in the community on which an expanding and mobile middle class could rely for fiction reading, for intellectual stimulation, and for meeting the knowledge requirements of a changing industrial economy. The scale and compactness of urban populations and the simplicity of industrial technologies before World War II made it possible for public libraries (as well as schools and research institutions) to meet demands placed upon them. The big city public libraries of the past did not have to be very large or especially sophisticated in storage systems or in personnel. Also the public library has always existed on a meager budget which, in many localities, amounted to what was left over after other municipal services got their own inadequate allotments. Private endowments have seldom provided much additional leeway in library budgets.

The big city libraries of the future will be diversified institutions responding to new demands, new opportunities, and new resources which are just beginning to be evident. A few will close their doors. In cities like Boston, where great private research libraries have flourished for a long time, the public libraries will, for the time being, concentrate their efforts in community service "out-reach" programs in neighborhood centers and mobile units among the underprivileged; free or low-priced nonreturnable paperbacks; greatly expanded preschool reading services; continuous showings of films; and perhaps lecture series shared by branch and suburban units through closed circuit television. Public libraries in cities like Boston will also be part of a metropolitan system capable of providing instantaneous printouts of specialized, annotated bibliographies showing the location of published and unpublished materials in all library collections in the metropolitan area, as well as in large national collections.

The public libraries in urban areas which lack accessible university research collections will develop a strong research capability. These libraries may even be the locus of the urban data banks now coming into being under the auspices of the U.S. Department of Housing and Urban Development.

Public libraries that develop as important research institutions (e.g., the New York Public Library) will also be obliged to serve the community. If this dimension is treated as a chore rather than as an opportunity, service may be correspondingly less imaginatively designed and less vigorously pursued than in those libraries where research is of minor importance.

Public research libraries will be the keystone institutions in the metropolitan systems of which they are a part. The systems led by research libraries are likely to be better integrated and technologically more sophisticated than those not research oriented. It may be that the research-oriented systems will service private industry directly through special contractual arrangements, especially if an urban data bank becomes part of the available service.

What I have described are prototypes of urban libraries and library systems. Actually, urban libraries in the future will fall along a continuum of these prototypes. Most big city libraries will be part of a metropolitan system, but not all the systems will operate effectively in serving the diverse and conflicting demands of metropolitan clientele. Some public libraries will cling to a parochial autonomy while going through the motions of cooperation. Some no doubt will resist technological innovation—but not many. The power of the federal dollar will win out, and high standards of planning and services will be developed and maintained.

It is inevitable that the greatest portion of public library funds in the years ahead will come from the federal government. The price of federal funds, even in conservative administrations, will be specialized services to the underprivileged and metropolitanwide organization of public library services. There is little doubt that most libraries will respond to these requirements (as many already have). The real question is whether librarians are prepared to respond.

We know that library administrators are not now appropriately trained to design and manage metropolitan systems. They know very little about the metropolitan demand structure for library and information services, the technological requirements of such services, and the problems of planning and coordination (let alone solutions). They have hardly begun to experience the problems of interjurisdictional politics which plague every effort in the no-man's-land of metropolitan planning and cooperation. Most white librarians are not yet psychologically or professionally prepared to deal effectively with problems of serving the deprived and excluded minorities. Adequate leadership of the public libraries of the future will require a drastic overhaul and broadening of the education of librarians coupled with the establishment of permanent library research and evaluation programs within library institutions.

Leaders in the library profession have to some extent recognized the need for changes in formal programs of education for librarians. Whether they have recognized the urgency of the need is hard for the outsider to judge, for changes in the curricula of library graduate schools are steadily taking place. Further steps in broadening these curricula must include urban sociology and urban planning, including the politics of planning in the American metropolis. Future library administrators must be expert in information science and in large-scale organizational management. They must also know the mission and capability of other institutions in the knowledge industry and how to adapt national goals and policies to regional and local needs. The big city and metropolitan librarian must be a skilled administrator of great executive capacity, a talented politician, an information specialist, and an egghead. The graduate schools of library science have the responsibility for meeting these formidable educational requirements. This objective could be served by encouraging students to take the relevant courses elsewhere in the university (as some do now) or by adding faculty to the library school staff who are specialists in the urban social sciences and in the management and information sciences.

Problems of market, management, and organization require continuous systematic attention in any public or private organization which has a responsibility either to itself or to a public to provide optimum service at an economical level. Discovering and defining one's market is an ongoing process, as is organization and management review. Problems of functional specialization, centralization versus decentralization, and organizational interrelations are classic in organizational planning. Continuous expert attention to these matters is a minimum requisite of organizational growth in response to new demands.

In order to meet these problems, individual libraries or groups of libraries should establish small, highly competent research and management teams to conduct a continuing review of the local market for library services; of the appropriateness of internal organizational structure; and of the character, quality, and relevance of services provided. These teams should also propose and help implement the development of network library systems, intergovernmental agreements, and other arrangements across jurisdictional lines.

Such teams would be a staff arm of large urban libraries or could serve as research staff to cooperating groups of libraries in metropolitan and rural areas. Their function should include collecting data for state and national library policy planning. Perhaps the local research teams should be components of a national research network largely supported by federal funds.

Permanent research teams in libraries would provide a nearly ideal place for some aspects of the training of future library administrators. In the training function, the teams would be the focus of an intellectual liaison between graduate library school faculties and library administrators, thus strengthening both institutions. They would also provide the American Library Association and its affiliates with ready-made local research units.

Several steps should be taken in the immediate future in preparation for meeting the requirements of planning metropolitan public libraries: (1) a prototype evaluation of present library services, programs, and facilities in the context of benefits to users and functions of other related institutions; (2) a prototype analysis of unmet needs of users and nonusers; (3) a prototype formulation of alternative ways of meeting needs through new or expanded programs and services and by developing locational, architectural, and organizational guidelines; and (4) a comprehensive evaluation of library education as administered by the graduate library schools.

How individual libraries respond to broadening opportunities for library services will be determined by the extent to which the present professional leadership adapts traditional modes to new challenges. The influential leadership is in the American Library Association, in the graduate library schools, in the federal Office of Education, and, to a lesser degree, in state libraries and the large urban libraries. The library profession is tightly organized, traditions are deeply rooted, and the methods of librarianship universally accepted and perpetuated. Personalities at senior levels play by the rules of the game; and even when they are vying for positions of influence, they preserve and reinforce the system.

These observations do, of course, apply to most professional groups. The closed system is functional in maintaining a disciplined standard of services, in controlling the quality of personnel who enter, and in shaping professional development to the standards of the system. These features are all to the good, provided they do not also function to shut out influences that would encourage vital adaptations to a changing environment. The points of entry of important new influences into the library profession are still extremely limited in spite of recent efforts of its more visionary leaders. Some of the entrenched professionals do not welcome new markets, new techniques, new approaches to traditional services, new patterns of institutional and interinstitutional organization, or even potential new sources of revenue.

A climate of receptivity to new influences will at best be a gradual development. A logical point of change is in the graduate library schools, where the capacity to tolerate new influences is bound to be the greatest in the profession. Steps to liberalize the formal education of library professionals and to put faculty into direct contact with other relevant disciplines will, in time, bring helpful influences to bear on change in the profession at large.

Another way to bring new influences into the profession would be to provide extensive mid-career opportunities for library administrators in fields outside traditional library training. There should also be annual programs for career librarians to take intensive courses in urban sociology, business management, planning, and the like.

The aim of such educational programs would be to broaden the perspective of library professionals and to acquaint them with the intellectual and practical tools of other disciplines. New perspectives and new tools will aid librarians in preparing their institutions for change and make it easier for senior professionals to accept the new product of a liberalized library school curriculum. In the long run, innovation in the education of librarians will be the key to the success of library institutions in meeting the imposing demands of the coming intellectual revolution.

NOTES

[1] Edward Banfield, *Urban Government: A Reader in Administration and Politics* (New York: Free Press, 1969), p.649.

FRANK S. MATHEWS

THE *Technological* ENVIRONMENT

A wise old Chinese philosopher who shall be nameless (mainly because I have never known his name) is reported to have said, "Only a fool makes predictions, particularly if they involve the future." Our purpose in meeting this morning is to examine the future, especially with respect to the effects of automation and technology on the culture and ultimately on the libraries of the seventies. Your speaker may be foolish in attempting to prognosticate, but your School of Librarianship committee which arranged for this Colloquium Series certainly was not foolish in its choice of time span. It would be very easy to foretell the events of, say, the twenty-first century. By the time all the rosy predictions had failed to materialize, you would all be either dead and buried, or at least widely dispersed and probably so senile that you would not even remember what was said here today. But by limiting our attentions to the seventies we are clearly on the spot! Such short-range predictions have a way of rising to haunt the one who prophesies.

Another philosopher who lived around 1000 B.C. wrote in the Proverbs of Solomon, "Where there is no vision the people perish." Perish the thought that we should perish for lack of vision! So there is nothing left to us but to grasp firmly our crystal ball (with which all good reference librarians come equipped these days) and, peering through the swirling mists of all the political, economic, and sociological un-

---

Dr. Mathews is professor of physics at the Colorado School of Mines and has received both Sigma Gamma Epsilon and Standard Oil Foundation awards for teaching excellence. With special interest in environmental and earth science, he heads the Committee on Environmental Factors in Mineral Engineering. He also serves as a consultant for the Westinghouse Geoscience Laboratory and the U.S. Geological Survey.

certainties of our day, deliver in clear and ringing tones unequivocal statements on the nature of the technological impacts on libraries in the next decade.

As I view the years ahead, I believe that technology will influence libraries in both a negative and a positive way. It will add heavy pressure to our library systems, but it will also help to relieve many pressures. It will make unprecedented demands on the systems, and then provide the means to meet these demands. It will prove to be at one and the same time not only a demanding taskmaster, but also a willing servant.

The pressures technology will bring to bear are threefold in character. In the first place, more and more of the scientific research being carried on these days is interdisciplinary in character. This increased interdisciplinary emphasis places increased demands upon reference librarians, because so many investigators are working in fields to which they are relative strangers. In the second place, the expansion of scientific knowledge and its codification into journal form have been growing exponentially for the last 220 years and show no signs of any slackening. This of course means that information storage and retrieval problems are also growing exponentially, even though library staffs do not always reflect the same growth rates. The third way in which technology will affect libraries will be through its influence on the leisure-time aspects of our culture.

Let us first examine in more detail the growth of the aforementioned interdisciplinary programs. The pressures and problems attendant on this growth are easily understood. In earlier times, science developed along quite traditional lines: mathematics, chemistry, physics, biology, and geology. As discoveries and insights in these disciplines came one after another in quick succession, the shadowy, ill-defined areas between these traditional, if somewhat arbitrarily defined, disciplines remained largely unexplored. More recently there has been a rush to explore these shadowy areas between the major disciplines. Much of the exciting research taking place today is in such fields: geochemistry, physical chemistry, geophysics, biophysics, and biochemistry. Although these fields are truly interdisciplinary, they are still sufficiently narrow in scope so that it has been possible to develop their own specialized journal literature reporting on research out to the very fringes of knowledge in these fields.

Still more recently, however, the growth of space exploration has resulted in a program so interdisciplinary in character that no one journal could possibly encompass all the subject matter. Furthermore, no one individual could hope to comprehend in any detail or even be familiar with the literature of the many disciplines which are sheltered under that single umbrella—space technology. The list is extensive. Mathematics, physics, chemistry, astronomy, cosmology, aerodynamics, civil engineering, mechanical engineering, electrical engineering, chemical engineering, medicine cryogenics, geodesy, geology, astrophysics—they are all here, and the geologist suddenly finds himself forced to rummage around in the esoteric and totally foreign literature of the astrophysicist. Fortunate indeed is the scientist with a skilled reference librarian to lead him by the hand through these strange mazes.

Finally, in 1971, we stand on the threshold of the greatest interdisciplinary adventure of all times. All the usual indicators—government funding, public pressures, political jockeying, and the exposures of everyday life—point to the fact that the 1970s will become *the decade of the environment*. Most of the mistakes that have been made thus far in environmental management have been sincere mistakes, but mistakes nevertheless because the decision-makers were considering too short a time span, too narrow a geographical perspective, or too narrow a technological viewpoint. Environmental decision-making in the seventies will require a much broader and more sophisticated perspective than has been possible heretofore. It will require teams of experts who are familiar with and can communicate in the subject matter of: economics, political science, sociology, demography, architecture, land planning, geography, geology, meteorology, hydrology, metallurgy, agriculture, forestry, biology, botany, ecology, medicine, seismology, cosmology, astronomy, all the traditional engineering fields, chemistry, physics, nuclear engineering, public health, mathematics, climatology, oceanography, bacteriology, and even theology and philosophy.

Insofar as a global overview of our environment is concerned, interactions between all these disciplines are possible. The list is endless. Hardly a major subject in the card catalogs is missing from the list of disciplines necessary for solving the environmental crisis. No single journal of environmental science can possibly encompass in sufficient detail all the disciplines needed. New methods of indexing and cross-referencing will need to be developed. Scientists will need to learn each other's specialized nomenclature and jargonese, develop a common technical language, study in each other's specialized journals, and become familiar with the bibliographic research tools of a wide variety of new subject areas. The cross-pollination of ideas and the new feedbacks developed between scientists who were hitherto strangers will be very exciting indeed. Obviously during such interactions, the demands on reference librarians will be greatly multiplied, and the reference librarian well versed in the needs of such interdisciplinary groups will make invaluable contributions to the research programs.

THE *Technological* ENVIRONMENT 23

The second technological pressure on libraries, that of the exponentially increasing demand for information storage and retrieval, has far more widespread implications and consequences. From a modest beginning of 10 scientific journals around the year 1730, the number of such journals has doubled approximately every fifteen years to a number presently in excess of 100,000. The number of abstract journals is also doubling every fifteen years, and presently stands at around 300, sufficiently large that a need for abstracts of abstracts is imminent. Projections based solely on past performance indicate that by the year 2000 A.D. the number of journals will be approaching the 1 million mark, and the number of abstract journals will probably exceed 2000.

Perhaps it would be useful for me to illustrate with an example just how inexorable the exponential growth function can be. The story is told of an Indian potentate who wished to reward one of his subjects for saving his life. "Ask what you will," said the potentate, "and I will give it." "Master," replied the subject, who was wise beyond his years, "my request is a simple one. You see this chessboard before us? I would merely like the wheat it takes if you give me one grain of wheat for the first square, two for the second square, four for the third square, eight for the fourth square, and so on, doubling the amount for each square until all sixty-four squares have been accounted for." "Granted!" exclaimed the potentate, gloating avariciously because he thought himself to have gotten off so lightly.

Imagine his chagrin when the payment of the reward began. 1, 2, 4, 8, 16, 32, 64, 128. Only 255 grains for the entire first row. 256, 512, 1024, 2048, 4096, 8192, 16,384, 32,768. A total of 65,536 grains (something like one pound of wheat) by the end of the second row. Now the exponential character of the doubling process begins to show itself with devastating suddenness. By the end of the third row the pile amounts to some 500 pounds of wheat. By the end of row number four the total is approaching 60 tons. Row number five sees the total in the neighborhood of 16,000 tons. By row number six the pile is over 4 million tons; by row seven, 500 million tons. To give you some idea of the enormity of this figure, this is enough wheat to cover the entire state of Colorado to a depth of several feet. Such is the nature of an exponential growth curve.

If scientific endeavor and publication follow a typical growth curve, one would expect the period of exponential growth to taper off eventually to a stable plateau. Such taperings off are not inevitable, however, since new techniques, processes, or developments can lead to a so-called "escalation" to a new exponential growth period. Price has suggested that finally, after more than 200 years of exponential growth, the onset of a tapering-off period in science may be almost upon us.

His premise is based on figures of research funding and percentages of national manpower engaged in research.[1] However, if the global rather than the national picture is considered, and if the remarkable efficiency of new devices and data acquisition techniques are recognized, it may very well be that we are entering an escalation to a new and even faster exponential rise rather than a tapering off. In any case, over just the next decade, even a transition to a tapering off would barely slow the accretion rate. It is of interest to note that the journal growth rates in China, USSR, Germany, and Japan far exceed the journal growth in the United States at the present time. The implications for the seventies in terms of foreign journal and journal-translation holdings are obvious.

Even though page costs are rising drastically and the average number of authors per journal article continues to increase, the number of journal articles and the number of journals still continues to rise exponentially. The implications of such growth are frightening. If retrieval techniques were to remain static, then the time to retrieve a given piece of information would increase exponentially during the seventies, or the probability of locating a given document would decrease exponentially. Coupled with the facts that retrieval of interdisciplinary information is inherently more involved than retrieval from well-defined disciplines and that the percentage of foreign journals searched is expected to rise, it is not too difficult to envision a time in the future when scientific discovery and development would either slow drastically or, on occasion, even grind to a halt because the rate of discovery would match the rate of nonretrieval of information lost in the vast journal depositories. I realize that these are fighting words to an assemblage of skilled librarians, but examples already abound of research repeated because the investigator was unaware of its prior disclosure.

Perhaps a personal example will illustrate what I mean. I recently had occasion to do some studies in the molten lava of a volcano. It was necessary to measure the electrical conductivity of this molten rock, and I therefore started checking to see whether such a measurement had ever been made or whether I could gain information about the process which would aid in the design of my instruments. My best efforts and those of several excellent reference librarians uncovered nothing in the literature which had any bearing on the subject. Only after my studies had been completed, and entirely by accident in connection with another study, I discovered two pieces of pertinent information: one in an obscure Czech journal of glass technology and the other in a Russian book on the chemistry of steel slags. If I found two valuable pieces of information by accident and in unexpected areas, how much information did I miss in other unexpected areas?

The third way in which technological developments will influence librarianship in the seventies will be through their influence on our leisure-time activities. By the middle of the seventies the four-day work week will be commonplace. If, as will be emphasized later, there is a growing need to de-emphasize the material aspects of our way of life, it is hoped that all segments of the population will discover a growing involvement with arts, crafts, and other aesthetic activities during the increased leisure. If the cultural aspects of life rather than mere entertainment become the focus of the newly acquired leisure, libraries can play a major role in stimulating and nurturing these interests.

Having painted a rather harried picture of the technological pressures on the libraries of the seventies, let us now examine some of the ways in which technology will help to relieve some of these pressures. Certainly the library automation trends already in evidence will accelerate, and most of the ordering, processing, circulating, and accounting activities of major libraries will be automated. The capabilities for such operations already exist. All that is needed now is money, and I believe one of your subsequent speakers will handle that problem.

The main way in which technology will impact on libraries will be in the area of information storage and retrieval. The very nature of the exponential growth curve of information suggests that the masses of data will soon become so huge that only high-density storage and automatic search techniques will be feasible. Technology will make major contributions to the solution of such storage and retrieval problems. It may be laser technology and its implications for optical scanning or data transmission; solid-state technology and its implications for more compact memories and improved access times; communications technology and its implications for long-distance data links and interlibrary hookups; or new software developments and their implications for the interfacing of many computers and many data banks. In a variety of ways, technology is contributing to the development of the fourth-generation computers of the seventies. With these fourth-generation computers, provided the megabucks are available, large-scale information storage and retrieval from entire collections or even lumped collections can become a reality.

The two main features of fourth-generation computers of interest for information storage and retrieval are: first, their large memories and, second, their fast access times. Peripheral to these features there are also the advantages of fast hard-copy printout and rapid long-distance data transmission.

Computer memories capable of storing all the world's journals are not yet available, but rapid progress is being made toward such a capability. New solid-state memories are providing storage capabilities far in excess of those of the more traditional core memories, and the new large-scale integrated circuits (LSI) give promise of extending storage capability still further, with the potential for even faster access times than are available in the best core memories. By 1975 access times are expected to fall well below fifty nanoseconds. Memories capable of storing a million abstracts are already available, and with the development of so-called "virtual memories," rapid-access units capable of storing over 30 million megabytes are being designed, with the only limitation to still further expansion being one of cost. There already exists the capability of virtually unlimited storage if slower access times are acceptable. Cost is the only limitation to the virtually unlimited proliferation of storage by means of magnetic tape or automated microfilm or microfiche systems. It is predicted that by the mid-seventies printers will become available capable of producing hard copy at the rate of 30,000 lines per minute. With the advent of laser communications and satellite relay technology, long-range data transmission systems will become available-capable of matching these rates.

Once rapid long-distance transmission of large masses of data becomes commonplace, the need for duplication of the very expensive massive data banks will disappear, and we will see the development either of gigantic regional data centers or groups of data centers, each with unique data and individual computers and interfaced by means of reliable, broad-band, long-distance data links. Evidence for the beginnings of such supersystems is already before us. Groups such as those of the General Electric Company and the Massachusetts Institute of Technology INTREX study are pioneering the investigation of new systems. Pilot programs supported by such diverse groups as the *New York Times,* the New York and American stock exchanges, various professional and scientific societies, and various government agencies are pointing the way to still larger, more complex, and more rapid systems. Typical of such systems is one in the planning stage by the U.S. Patent Office. It is capable of storing complete information including facsimiles for over 10 million patents. Storage capability is 20 billion on-line characters and 600 billion off-line.

Key to the entire retrieval problem is the effective design of descriptors. The lava-glass-slag example mentioned earlier illustrates perfectly how useful data can be overlooked for lack of adequate descriptors. It is my own personal conviction that no journal article should be published without its associated descriptors. These should be chosen by the author himself, in consultation with a skilled retrieval specialist.

By the late seventies we should be seeing the development of the aforementioned massive data centers with rapid-access storage of all abstracts and descriptors, and off-line storage of the textual material. Rapid data links should permit the interfacing of several of these centers, and rapid readout and printout devices should make hard copy readily available. Conceivably, abstract readout should be available within seconds, and hard-copy printout within minutes in all major libraries in the country.

Having extrapolated our present technology and culture into and through the seventies, let us pause a moment and consider where our extrapolations will lead us. At the onset I promised you that I would not paint a rosy picture of the future. I would now like to spell out in more detail the causes for my pessimism. Perhaps between the black brush strokes of today's lecture and the white brush strokes of Dr. Conant's lecture last month, you will be able to arrive at a valid consensus.

Everything we have anticipated thus far has been predicated on a continuation or even an expansion of our present technology. Yet it is this very technology which is coming under more and more violent attack by conservation groups, environmental protection groups, concerned politicians, and that segment of the population which Reich in *The Greening of America* labels Consciousness III.[2] The problems of pollution and environmental degradation have been examined from many points of view, and a variety of panaceas have been proposed. In one way or another, most of the suggested cures result in the consumer's ultimately bearing the cost of the cleanup. And herein lies the rub! Any increase in the cost of living will automatically bring cries for increased wages, which in turn can only be satisfied if industry increases production and creates additional markets. But the U.S. economy is already geared to the treadmill of increasing production in order to fill artificially created demands, and any so-called "cure" which entails an increased consumption of energy and raw materials automatically worsens the environmental degradation. The only way off the vicious treadmill is for the American consumer voluntarily to settle for a drastically lowered material standard of living.

The problem can best be seen in perspective if one considers the resources of the globe as a whole. At the present time the United States is consuming far more than her share of the world's resources. With only 6 percent of the world's population, she nevertheless consumes some 50 percent of the nonrenewable resources expended each year. At the same time that the United States is consuming global resources at such an appalling rate, she is also exporting her technology and know-how to the undeveloped nations by means of agencies such as AID, UNESCO, and the Peace Corps. It is only a matter of time before the standard of living and the degree of industrialization of these nations begin to improve, and the nations begin to demand their fair share of the world's nonreplenishable resources.

When such a time arrives (and it cannot be too far distant), only two options remain. The United States can either opt to exploit the remaining resources at a still greater rate (to the eternal loss of our grandchildren), or she can cut her consumption of nonrenewable resources from 50 percent to her fair 6 percent share. Such a cut would suggest a cut in living standards by a factor of 8. The blow might be lessened by improved production techniques, recycling of used materials, and development of substitute materials, but a reduction in the standard of living by a factor of at least 2 appears inevitable. Quite frankly, while my idealistic self cries "this *must* be," my pragmatic self looks at human nature, and particularly the human nature of the average American consumer, and cries "this can never be."

Herein lies the dilemma. Technology has apparently subverted itself to the place where its inevitable dissolution or at least retrenchment is assured. The only questions really remaining are "how" and "when."

Before the picture becomes too gloomy, let me hasten to add a pair of bright touches: one involving technology and one involving people. Technologically, very active research programs in Great Britain, the United States, and the USSR are exploring the feasibility of harnessing the nuclear fusion process for the commercial production of power. There have been many discouraging failures and some brilliant successes. Should fusion power become commercially available in time to meet the environmental pressures, there is enough energy available in the heavy hydrogen of the oceans to solve the world's environmental problems for thousands of generations. With an essentially limitless source of energy the world's wastes could all be recycled; the world's atmosphere, rivers, and oceans could all be scrubbed clean; and the depletion of our fossil fuels would be no tragedy at all.

There is hope, too, in the attitudes and values of the people of this land. The members of the Counter Culture have had an influence on our nation out of all proportion to their numbers. I suspect that there is more than a little of Consciousness III in each of us. With the passing years our perception of reality continually undergoes subtle shifts, so that our views on the corporate state and the public state; on wealth, clothing, and goods; on work and technology; on human dignity, truth, and beauty change. Perhaps they will have changed sufficiently by the time the "crunch" comes that we will accept the dematerialism almost gaily as being merely the natural and desirable order of things. If the confrontation were to occur with my generation, I fear the consequences would be disastrous. If it occurs with the generation now in college, perhaps the confrontation will scarcely be noticeable.

What I have been saying is not to suggest that during the seventies the dissolution of technology and the environment will occur. Rather it sets the stage, so that as the precursors of these developments begin to surface in the seventies, they may be recognized and placed in their proper perspective. The coming decade should still be one of rapid technological advance. The rate of production of information should continue to accelerate. The establishment of gigantic regional information depositories should become a reality. The rate of retrieval and dissemination of information should improve markedly. Professional journals may begin to be seen less and less by library patrons, and librarians will most certainly be exposed to computer technology in ever increasing doses. All in all, it should be an exciting decade, and one in which we certainly are all fortunate to be living.

NOTES

[1] Derek J. DeSolla Price, *Science since Babylon* (New Haven, Conn.: Yale University Press, 1961).

[2] Charles A. Reich, *The Greening of America* (New York: Random House, 1970), p.222.

RALPH E. ELLSWORTH

THE *Institutional* ENVIRONMENT

I should like to begin by quoting from a letter from a faculty member at the University of Chicago to a friend of mine. It concerns the new University of Chicago Library building, and it says a great deal about modern buildings in a very few words:

> The Joseph Regenstein Library opened for business in October. It is the largest, most impressive and most expensive building on the campus. It is so impressive that I decided to use it for my Xmas card and give the perennial partridge a rest.
>
> The exterior walls are formed by deeply grooved, sawn limestone slabs. And that is only one of the reasons why the building is so groovy.
>
> The interior is enormous, with few partitions and obstructions. The floors are carpeted wall to wall in gold. Gold velvet arm chairs so comfortable that you fall asleep in them are all about. I predict that the scholarly output and input of faculty and students will decrease fifty percent in the coming year.
>
> Each study table is enclosed on three sides so that you hear no evil and see no evil. Over the table in the form of a drawer is a locker providing an ideal place for planting time bombs.
>
> There are seven floors of stack acres in extent. Readers are free to enter, but they are frisked when they come out. You must come and see it. But you had better come soon for it may be blown up at any moment.

Dr. Ellsworth has been director of libraries at the University of Colorado since 1958. He is president of the Association of College and Reference Libraries and a recognized authority on library facilities for educational institutions.

Before we begin speculating about the future physical environment of libraries, we should properly pay tribute to changes made since World War II in building planning that made it possible for the University of Chicago to have a library with the qualities described in the letter. Almost without exception the library buildings more than twenty-five years old were formal, austere, impersonal, cold—physically and psychologically—and puritanical in their provisions for the comfort of readers. They seldom included provisions for readers to study among the books; they seldom could be reorganized to meet the needs of new activities; they seldom could be enlarged to maintain a unified library program.

Today the opposite of each of these statements holds for almost all new academic and public libraries. Indeed there are many buildings so glamorous their publics can hardly ignore them.

The planning of library buildings has become so much a part of the life of chief librarians it sometimes seems the buildings are more important than the libraries inside them. In fact, today *there is a disturbing parallel between the church and the library* in terms of their physical environments.

Obviously the church is a place where religious activities are practiced. The building houses these activities but is not of itself religious. The silver chalices, the velvet gowns, the icons play a symbolic role in the life of the church, but they of themselves are not religious. The religious life could be practiced in a desert without any of the church trappings; and if I read the mood of the youth today correctly, they are attempting to do just that.

The library building houses library activities but is not of itself a library. The structure, the furniture, the carpets, the electronic and audiovisual hardware all play a useful role, but they have no real importance in their own right qua librarianship. When universities spend $18 million to $25 million on a library building to house an activity that could be housed in a $5 million structure, one may properly ask if librarians may not be guilty of the same faults that religious leaders are in confusing the building with the activities that go on inside.

Why is it we librarians have become so much interested in the physical plants that house our libraries? Could it be because of:

The symbolism of the library. Ever since man began to be able to accumulate knowledge, knowledge has represented power. Since the development of the atomic bomb and Sputnik, man's respect for knowledge has taken a quantum jump. Notice today our use of the phrase, "Well, if we can place a man on the moon, surely we can _____ _____ _____." Then you fill in whatever you think we ought to be able to do. The respect for knowledge as power tends to rub off on the house where knowledge lives, just as in the case of the church the religious mood and practice rub off on the church building and the icons used in religious services. Thus, we give the library the most impressive site on the campus, and we insist that it have an impressive or monumental exterior.

The memorial idea. You've noticed, haven't you, how many of our library buildings are named after a person? How better to perpetuate oneself and at the same time help mankind in a useful way than to give money for a library building?

The new building technology and the abundance of beautiful things to live with. Artificial light, air conditioning, carpeting, wonderful colors, comfortable furniture, great art, etc., all these we expect to find in our library buildings. Our public delights in giving us money with which to purchase these beautiful things.

My parallel continues. People *could* practice religion without a church building or a religious organization to promote religion, but experience tends to show that they don't. They might for a while, but people need a kind of *religious information-switching center* between themselves and their idea of God.

Likewise one can argue that with our new electronic and other communication technology—television, the computer, facsimile transmission, microforms, etc.—people *could* have access to the contents of carriers of information without ever coming into a library building. The library could become merely an *information-switching center* between the person and the great banks of knowledge. This may happen to libraries, and indeed it has already begun to happen in academic libraries. For example:

The paperback book. Although we now take the paperback for granted, we should remember that it is most revolutionary in its effect on library use. Students expect nowadays to buy the texts of the belles lettres and other books that they formerly had to come to the library to borrow.

Xerox copying machine. Why sit in a library reading a journal article when you can make a copy of it and read it in comfort in your room with a can of beer in one hand, one eye on the article, and the other on the television screen?

Faculty nonuse. We seldom see members of the faculty in university libraries anymore because we have lessened their need to come there by:

1. *Faculty delivery service.* Our faculty can call up the library, and we will deliver the book immediately and pick it up when they are through with it.

2. *Current awareness services.* Tables of contents of the new journals plus lists of newly arrived books, plus automatic procurement plans, such as the Abel Plan, enable faculty to stay in their offices, studios, or laboratories and telephone the library for the materials they need to read from these lists and services.
3. *Library searching.* Projects such as the Educational Resources Information Center (ERIC) Clearinghouse for Social Science Education are busy assembling, in microfiche form, scattered information for teachers. Like the yellow pages doing your leg work, these projects do your library searching. You have more time to be an educator.
4. *Computerized circulation systems.* The one at Ohio State can be consulted by telephone to find instantly the availability and whereabouts of library materials, thus enabling the faculty to avoid going to the library.
5. *The availability of grant money.* Such funds have enabled our best scholars to assemble in their offices the material they need for research without waiting for the cumbersome library establishment to procure it, organize it, and prepare it for use.

These ideas or projects are today having the effect of enabling faculty to do their work without coming into the library building at all.

All these developments except (1) and (2) are very expensive, and they do change the patterns of library use for faculty, but not necessarily for students. For the foreseeable future, students apparently will be present in our academic libraries in increasing numbers. The things we now do to make them comfortable, as was stated in the letter describing the University of Chicago Library, all help make them want to study in the library even though it has nothing to do with the process of transferring the contents of library materials from the books into the readers' minds.

I have carried the parallel between the church and the library as far as I dare, and I will now comment on other developments in academic libraries that affect their physical environment. First, the concept of the library as primarily an information-dispensing center and less as a book handler of the carriers of information it houses alters its space priorities. Subject information specialists need not just a desk out in the reading room but large workrooms in which they can handle, absorb, and relate information to students and faculty. These librarians need support staffs of varying levels to do the leg work. They require not just the 110 assignable square feet allowed by state officials but a suite of rooms equipped with photocopying machines, computer terminals, cassette copiers, tape copiers, video tape recorders, and all the other new technology of communications. There must be library subject information specialists to cover *all* the curricular departments in the university, not just the humanities as has been true in past years.

Second, the size of the so-called reference materials collection has increased and will continue to do so until and if much of this material is put on the computer and ways of financing the use of the computer are available. These possibilities seem a long way off in terms of the cost elements. So I anticipate that we will continue to acquire the G. K. Hall catalogs of other libraries and the *National Union Catalog* and a great many other tools that we now buy at a very high cost in order to locate materials in other libraries. Such projects as the computerized federal census data are beyond the pocketbook levels of most of us. So is the *Chemical Abstracts* retrieval system at $12,000 a year. Yet the information our scholars need is available through these technological means. The only question is one of finance or, as one might say, the economics of information dispensing.

Third, architects apparently are the most insecure of all professionals. They are faddist addicts. First it was glass walls and then no windows. Next it is atriums in the middle of our buildings, and then it is a reversion to the tower concept of libraries. Now it is wide, low, underground platforms with balls of various shapes placed on top. Or if architects are required to make fenestration functional, that is, minimal, in most of the building, they insist on reserving the right to use glass walls on the main floor. So, like the Victorian female, the building is restricted at the main-floor level so that the overhang keeps the sun out.

This means that there isn't room on the main floor for everything the librarians think should go there. So we now move the technical processes to another floor or even out of the building, and we find much to our amazement that this can be done—thanks to oral and visual communication technology—without a major loss in staff time. There is one drawback—it does destroy the concept of merging the traditional reference and technical processing staffs into subject information specialists working closely with teaching faculty.

Fourth, apparently the enrollment growth of colleges and universities is to be stabilized, and the needs of an increasing population are to be met, not by allowing existing institutions to grow but by creating more colleges and universities (even though today we hear that the private colleges, at least many of them, will have to close for lack of money). But no one knows if a larger percentage of high school students in this country will go to college; and if so, to what kind of a college and where will these colleges be located? So in terms of librarians trying to anticipate and calculate the reader station needs of the future, the situation is impossible. Library buildings that cannot be enlarged and reorganized to meet new conditions will be white elephants on their campuses. This applies both to the structure itself, to the site problem, and to the problem of architectural harmonies with adjacent buildings.

In terms of space for book growth, the trends are running in varying directions:

1. More books, journals, and other media are bought each year at an increased cost but with declining budgets; more books are available in microforms but usually are marketed unrealistically by firms such as Encyclopaedia Britannica who package their wares with Adlerian theology, inadequate hardware, and titles we don't much need anyway.
2. We don't really know how best to make multimillion volume collections easily available to scholars. Storage of little-used books sounds great, but notice that universities like Chicago, Michigan, and the University of California at Berkeley plan on bringing back into their new central buildings the books they were storing off campus once these new buildings are finished.
3. On the older university campuses the academic buildings are seldom placed where their faculties can work closely with their colleagues in related disciplines in the new intellectual constellations. The new universities that are planning buildings adaptable to more than one departmental function may survive; the older universities may not. So it is with library buildings.
4. In contemplating the future of our buildings we must realize that the college and university campus as we know it today *could disappear* as a result of the improvements our schools have already made and are capable of making in the future and as a result of the application of electronic technology.

If you will consider for a minute the share of each individual's life required to prepare himself for participation in living in the skilled and professional occupations in earlier societies with that required for living in our society, you will realize that over a third of a person's life can be spent in preparation. Ask yourself how great a share of its wealth can a society afford to put into the preparation process.

It may well be that after the period of secondary education (much improved, of course), preparation for the professions will be decentralized and students will spend much of their time off campus working, perhaps as an apprentice and taking classes by television as they are doing at Colorado State University and other universities today.

The role of the library might change in part from that of a study center to that of preparing prepackaged kits of information for off-campus use. It is doubtful if this change would affect the research activities of universities, but it could affect undergraduate and professional education. The beginnings of the trend are present. They may or may not develop.

Thus far colleges and universities have operated like medieval baronies without regard to the needs, the welfare, and the financial-support capacities of geographic areas of the country. Look, if you please, at the curricular offerings of the state-supported and other privately supported universities in the Rocky Mountain region or even in Colorado as a state. If you can see any logic or even any sanity in this picture, you should speak up. Witness the spokesmen for public- and private-supported colleges defending their positions by trotting out clichés and stereotypes about quality levels, the advantages of small or large classes, the advantages of private boards of control versus public boards, their innovative role, etc., and you will witness more high-class deception than you will find in the typical TV ad for automobiles or deodorants.

Naturally our campus physical plants reflect this local concept of sovereignty. How many schools of mines or forestry do the Rocky Mountain states really need? Do all universities have to engage in research in the same fields of science just because one of them does? Do both Colorado University and Colorado State University need research institutes for alpine studies? I suggest that this kind of competition has ended. A library in a university for tomorrow ought to have a helicopter port on top or in its back yard, and it should plan on being able to move books, faculty, and even students among campuses to make the best possible use of all three kinds of resources. Our materials collections should be gathered and organized on the assumption that on the basis of joint planning and joint borrowing we will be able to bring into the state a larger number of materials our scholars need than we did in the days when we operated independently of one another. If we can promise twenty-four-hour delivery service (and how many of us do better than that today?), supplemented by systems of instant access to text by electronics, we could do a rational job of planning our book-collection growth and the buildings in which they are to be kept.

We have known this truth for a long time, but we have done nothing about it. It may turn out that we librarians will someday wear Saint Nixon badges around our necks to express our appreciation for the fact that the President's economic policies deprived us of income to the point where we had to go about organizing our library economies in a sensible manner, and to bring about the reforms we talked about but never did anything about as long as we had too much money to afford making the changes.

There have been many variations on the theme of the *library-college*, some wise and sensible, some quite silly. But under the label of independent study and special honors and other individual curriculum patterns, we are indeed coming close to the library-college idea.

Its future will depend pretty much on the success the lower schools have not only with motivating their students more vigorously but also with acquainting them with the habits of independent study. The conditions are favorable. Should this idea take hold, the implications for academic library buildings are simply that we shall all need more of the best kinds we have today. So much for colleges and universities.

In the lower schools the future has already become the present. Visit, if you please, the Clear Creek County High School in Idaho Springs, and you will see there the living example of a library that became a school and a school that became a library. You can now see this in many elementary and secondary schools in the country. I saw it ten years ago in the Ifield Junior School in Crawley-New-Town, England and I have helped plan three such libraries in the United States.

The idea is simply to make it possible for each child, under careful guidance, to take the initiative for his learning efforts insofar as he or she can learn to do this. Many books, tools, studio and laboratory equipment, audiovisual media, etc., are dispersed throughout the building on a completely integrated (not separate but equal) basis, because all parts of the school become places where students learn. And not just learning materials; people from the community who have something to contribute—carpenters, lawyers, merchants, journalists, ministers, artists, social workers—come and go and are available as learning resources to work with students. The school and the community begin to pull together in a manner so that the student begins to relate the things he learns from books to the kind of life he finds in his community.

Librarians indeed are present, and they have to work very much harder than they did in the past. They sometimes carry the title of Media Specialists (reflecting the fact that many of the things we librarians do seem mysterious to outsiders) or Learning Materials Specialists, and they carry the awesome responsibility for helping teachers and students decide which learning materials are most helpful for the task in hand. In this respect I should have mentioned that I have never yet met a university librarian who was enthusiastic about organizing books and other media on a *fully integrated basis*. Quite a few are satisfied with the concept of *separate but equal* treatment, but no one to my knowledge, with one exception, has gone further than that.

The physical chaos one finds in these schools or libraries is wonderful, and so is the amount of learning going on there. When the graduates of these schools hit the campuses, I predict they will tear the place apart and retire most of the faculty. The library physical plant in these schools involves more than just the central reference center, which does exist. The library is infused throughout the entire school building. It comes as close to being a bibliothecal heaven on earth as most of us will ever see.

I prefer not to say much about the physical plant future of other-type libraries, public and special, because I know too little about them. I have visited many of the new public library systems, and it is obvious that they bear no resemblance to the buildings of the pre-World War II era. They are designed to attract readers, to make their reading experiences more interesting and comfortable, and to help them relate their reading to their own personal and community experiences. If one could substitute the word campus for city or county, I think the future purposes and activities of public and academic libraries would turn out to be somewhat similar except that the range of demand in the public library field would be wider than in the universities, especially at the children's end for the public library and the research end for the university.

If I were to coin a phrase to express a key note for the library buildings of the future, I would say (and indeed I have said so before) that the library house of the future is a home in which it is possible for the librarian to come out of the kitchen and to drink with the guests in the parlor.

DAVID H. CLIFT

THE *Organizational* ENVIRONMENT

I have been asked to discuss with you today the organizational environment of library associations; the role of such organizations at the national, regional, and state levels; the problems resulting from the proliferation of organizations based on special-interest groups and divergent goals; and the structure and relevancy of library organizations.

The dictionary speaks of *environment* as meaning "the aggregate of all the external conditions and influences affecting the life and development of an organism. . . . " It also mentions *environment* as meaning "surroundings." Certainly, one could describe the American Library Association as currently being surrounded by many internal and external forces and points of view. For what comfort it may be worth, forces and points of view have on several past occasions also surrounded the association.

The American Library Association has been in existence since 1876. Throughout its life, it has been constantly engaged in self-examination of its purpose and its structure. These examinations have been conducted in several ways, usually by activities committees from the membership.[1] There has been one overall and thorough study by a management firm[2] and separate studies of different units by members and by outside firms. It could be said, then, that the association has rigorously examined itself on an average of once every fifteen years. The present association has evolved from this continued study by members and by persons and agencies from outside the organization.

Mr. Clift has served as executive director of the American Library Association since 1951. In addition to previous positions at Yale and Columbia, he has been a consultant to the U.S. government on library affairs and an active participant in numerous library and educational organizations.

Briefly, the present structure of the association is: a grouping of members into fourteen divisions, each with a governing board; committees for ALA as a whole and committees within the divisions; round tables, for discussion purposes, with a membership smaller than the divisions; a Council, which is the governing body of the association, with a present voting membership of 217 plus approximately 31 nonvoting members; and a fourteen-member Executive Board, which is the administrative arm of the Council. There are also chapters, these being the state and regional library associations.[3]

The Council meets twice each year, at the Midwinter Meeting and the Annual Conference, for a total of approximately twelve to fifteen hours. There are also meetings of the membership in attendance at the Annual Conference. The membership can, under present provisions, meet at times other than the Annual Conference if called for by petition or by action of the Executive Board.

In order that we may better understand the legislative workings of the association, you must understand the responsibilities and authority of the ALA Council and the membership. The membership's conclusions and actions constitute recommendations to the officers and to Council, and the membership can require Council to respond within a stated period. Council is the governing body of the association and, as such, determines the policies of the association. The membership can, either by action at a meeting or by a mail vote of the entire membership, set aside a decision of Council.

It may be useful, at this point, to describe something of Council's operations in the past. The Council is a large body. It has not always been thoroughly informed on the matters coming before it, partly because the needed information cannot always be provided in advance and partly because the members of Council have not always informed themselves when advance information was provided.

As a consequence, the Council has been viewed by some as a rubber stamp, quickly accepting a recommendation accompanying any proposal. This is untrue since the Council often gives thorough and thoughtful consideration to issues of great concern to the association. Examples that can be mentioned are the debates within Council on federal support of education, intellectual freedom, and organization of the association.

It might be said that sometimes the Council has shown an inaccurate understanding of the wishes of the membership. This was particularly demonstrated by its action, twice within the past fifteen years,[4] in favor of moving headquarters from Chicago to Washington—actions which the membership promptly overruled.

It is interesting, also, to point out reasons for the often diverse actions of the membership and Council. First, neither body meets often enough to become fully familiar with the issues under discussion. The Council does not have internal working committees, and it must consider all matters as sort of a committee of the whole. Since neither body is fully informed, each sometimes acts out of emotion. The result could be loosely characterized by saying that the membership often goes overboard in its recommendations while the Council often reacts in a conservative manner. The two bodies, in many ways, offer commendable checks and balances.

Let's discuss, then, the organizational environment in which ALA has found itself from 1968 to the present. In considering these efforts for change, I shall deal principally with the activities and interests of chapters; the Social Responsibilities of Libraries Round Table; the Activities Committee on New Directions for ALA, known as ACONDA and started by a membership meeting; the Ad Hoc Council Committee to Work with ACONDA, now known as ANACONDA; and the membership and Council. Insofar as is possible and clear, I'll take the actions of these groups in sequence. Let me, also, relieve others of responsibility. Many of the comments on the association represent a personal view.

Let's begin with the chapters of ALA. Do these chapters, the state and regional library associations, as part of ALA exert any unifying influence? A quick answer is "Yes, to some extent"—simply because they exist. A far more exact answer is that they do not exert to the full any unifying influence.

There have been occasions when the interest in a subject has caused the programs of ALA to be reflected in programs of action by the state and regional associations. Special and continuing interest has existed in the areas of legislation (the libraries received tangible benefits here); intellectual freedom (the apprehensive, as well as the dedicated, found a rallying point); the report of the present and past activities committees of ALA (the present committee, particularly right now, because its recommendations would deprive the chapters of representation in Council); and the frequently expressed need for a national placement service (again, something for the members).

Let me bring the frame of reference down to Colorado, and I admit to you that I speak without any certain knowledge of the Colorado Library Association. I could just as easily present these questions to the Illinois or the Kentucky or the Connecticut Library Association. But let me put several situations to you as members of the Colorado Library Association or as persons with a commitment to librarianship:

1. Do you read—and make yourself familiar with—the agenda before the meeting?

2. Do you express your concerns to the persons who have an obligation to speak for you?
3. What are your motivating concerns in seeking information: personal, parochial, or professional?
4. Do you read the literature on the subject of your interests?
5. Do you make suggestions for your association to consider?
6. Finally—are you a member? Do you vote?

Second, let me ask some questions of those—if any are present—who are engaged in planning the activities of library associations:

1. How well do you understand the needs and wants of your members? When did you last endeavor to find out what kinds of activities are of most concern to them?
2. Do you give priority in planning your annual conferences to social activities only?
3. How far does the conception of your responsibility to the state library association extend? To the annual meeting only? To increasing membership? To finding out and meeting needs?
4. How do you attract new members? By simply mailing a dues notice? By planning substantive programs?
5. How much thought have you given to effective and needed programs on library education, bibliographical control, reaching the nonusers of libraries, shared personnel, to name a few?

Let me here recommend one item, at least, that you might read and ponder on this subject. It is *The Southwestern Library Association Project Report: ALA Chapter Relationships—National, Regional, and State*. This is a study financed by a J. Morris Jones–World Book Encyclopedia–ALA Goals Award and carried out under the perceptive, hard-hitting, no-holds-barred direction of Grace Thomas Stevenson, formerly deputy executive director of ALA. No stranger to the foibles and fancies of library associations of whatever level, Mrs. Stevenson describes well—and prescribes well—for ALA and state and regional library associations. Her study will, I'm sure, make you think hard concerning your own association. She reports, for instance:

> The most impressive fact which came out of this study was the evidence that many librarians know so little about their professional associations at any level, state, regional, or national. The result is confusion, frustration, and dissatisfaction—members and nonmembers unhappy with their associations because they do not understand their purposes nor how to use them. All of the library

associations need to design and use continuously a program of information about their objectives, structure, and program. The concomitant is the obligation on the part of librarians to inform themselves about their associations, both for their own advancement and that of the profession and library service.

Much in her report is aimed directly at ALA. She also writes:

> There is much [concerning chapters] besides their place in the structure that needs discussion between ALA and its chapters— the allocation and responsibility for programs; the ever-recurring request for regional meetings; the possibility of regional ALA offices . . . the [need for] a Chapter Relations Office at Headquarters. The ALA structure should provide an opportunity for continuing discussion with the chapters of such concerns.

All this and much more than could be quoted seem to indicate clearly that much is amiss with all our associations: national, regional, and state. I can think of many means that might be used to improve the situation. I think I know where the eventual answers will be found. They will come from persons who are in this room and many more like you in library schools spread across the country. I suspect, also, that the answer lies somewhere between Francis Bacon's ringing statement and the questing and groping concerns of today's young librarians. Bacon wrote, you will recall:

> I hold every man a debtor to his profession; from the which as men of course do seek to receive countenance and profit, so ought they of duty to endeavour themselves, by way of amends, to be a help and ornament thereunto.[5]

The young members of our profession are asking, I think, questions which ought to be answered: How relevant are associations to the profession and to the lives we lead? How can associations advance the public good in a time of war and in times when to stand up and be counted in the fight for intellectual freedom may mean one more entry in the Positions Wanted column?

The efforts for change in ALA began with groups unaffiliated formally with ALA. These groups identified themselves as "321.8" and the "Congress for Change." From these groups—or because of them— came the ALA Round Table on the Social Responsibilities of Libraries. It is interesting to note that the round table rather consistently refers to itself as the Social Responsibilities Round Table, thus dropping any reference in its title to libraries.

The idea of a round table on the social responsibilities of libraries was approved at a meeting of the membership in Kansas City on 26 June 1968.[6] This proceeded from a petition of nearly 300 members. The membership meeting at that Annual Conference took action that day and

> VOTED, That the Membership instructs Council to request the Committee on Organization to report to the Executive Board their recommendation for or against the establishment of a Round Table on the Social Responsibilities of Libraries, and That the action of the Committee on Organization and of the Executive Board be reported to Council at its meeting on Friday, June 28, 1968.

Council was, properly I think, unable to move as fast as the instruction from membership requested and voted, instead,

> That the Committee on Organization report to the Executive Board their recommendation for or against the establishment of a Round Table on the Social Responsibilities of Libraries, and That the action of the Committee on Organization and of the Executive Board be reported to Council expeditiously.

The presiding officer stated that the word *expeditiously* would be taken seriously and that action would come within a reasonable length of time.

This same Council meeting at the 1968 Annual Conference considered another resolution from the membership meeting that is pertinent to our subject today. It would have required platform statements from the candidates for the office of first vice-president (and president-elect) and second vice-president, the statement to be distributed with the ballots. There was brief discussion centering around the political-campaign atmosphere this might produce, and the motion was defeated. A later meeting of Council (Midwinter 1970) accepted the proposal and

> VOTED, That the ALA ballots for the positions of councilor and president be accompanied by a short statement of the candidates' professional concerns.

A word on the 1968 Annual Conference. There was a lot of talk about the "generation gap." The editor of the *ALA Bulletin* commented on the source of this talk:

> Men shiny of pate, grey of lock, and wrinkled of brow were intoning threats of doom to those they felt had shinier heads, greyer hair, and deeper crow's-feet. The truly young, however, were seemingly more interested in learning how their association works, and how they can have a voice in its affairs. That was the true importance of the Kansas City [Conference] of 1968.[7]

It seemed clear to all that participation was far more stimulating than observation.

The Committee on Organization did move expeditiously in its study of the proposed Round Table on the Social Responsibilities of Libraries and was able to complete its study and recommend establishment of the round table to Council at the 1969 Midwinter Meeting. Council approved and accepted the purposes of the round table as follows:

> To provide a forum for the discussion of the responsibilities of libraries in relation to the important problems of social change which face institutions and librarians; to provide for exchange of information among all ALA units about library activities with the goal of increasing understanding of current social problems; to act as a stimulus to the Association and its various units in making libraries more responsive to current social needs; to present programs, arrange exhibits, and carry out other appropriate activities.

The Congress for Change held a meeting in June of 1969. On 19 June, nearly 180 persons, predominately from library schools and from the New York, Pennsylvania, and Maryland areas met in Washington, D.C. The idea for this meeting came from an earlier meeting of "concerned students." The Washington meeting discussed the shortcomings of the organized profession of librarianship and concluded it would present a program at the ALA membership meeting on 23 June 1969 in Atlantic City. At that meeting the group made a number of statements. Marching to the microphone near the speaker's platform, they presented their case as follows:

1. The first speaker discussed *change* in the association. Unless the group's demands for change were met, she stated, they would discourage membership in ALA.
2. A second speaker went to the subject of intellectual freedom (this was considered further by the membership meeting of that week). Her proposal called for additional staff, adequate funds including support funds, and the establishment of sanctions. (This was followed by a proposal to Council that week by the Intellectual Free-

dom Committee for a program of action, which set forth how the IFC would proceed in cases involving intellectual freedom, and this was approved by Council.)
3. Next to the microphone came a speaker on library education. This speaker read a statement on reform in library education and moved its adoption. The statement included transferring the accreditation of library school programs out of ALA into the Association of American Library Schools. The membership meeting removed this recommendation, and the Council at the Midwinter Meeting 1970 referred the entire matter to the Office for Library Education.
4. Another speaker presented a resolution suggesting that the 1970 Midwinter Meeting not be held in Chicago. The resolution failed to pass the membership by a vote of 578 to 299.
5. A rather lengthy statement was then read on the antiballistic missile system. There were objections to the language, and the motion failed by a vote of 216 to 183.
6. A nonmember of ALA then read a statement condemning the war in Vietnam. This eventually reached the floor in the form of a motion duly presented. There was lengthy debate, and finally, very late in the afternoon, a motion was passed 345 to 131 "that those present go on record against the war in Vietnam."

SRRT (Round Table on the Social Responsibilities of Libraries) moved ahead with its organizational matters. At a meeting in June of 1969, it began to set up its organization and procedures, with consideration of a document entitled "Organization and Procedure." The organization was to be based on aggressive volunteers, and all nominations to office within SRRT would come from volunteers. Two elected committees would serve the round table for the purpose of coordinating the round table's task forces. It was proposed by a speaker at this same meeting that librarians abandon ALA and form their own association. Another speaker suggested that ALA become an association of librarians only.

The Atlantic City Conference in June of 1969 saw also the authorization of the Activities Committee on New Directions for ALA. This was proposed in the membership meeting on June 25, and the motion directed the ALA president to establish the committee, which came to be known as ACONDA, as soon as practicable. ACONDA was to include thirteen members: three to come from six nominations submitted by the Junior Members Round Table, three to come from six nominations submitted by SRRT, seven including the chairman to be selected by the president. The intent here was to have a mixture of the young and not-so-young. The committee was to meet as often as necessary. It was to submit an interim report of progress at the 1970 Midwinter Meeting and a final report at the 1970 Annual Conference. The committee, in the course of its study, was:

> To recognize the changes in the interests of ALA members and provide leadership and activities relevant to those interests
>
> To reinterpret and restate the philosophy of ALA in order to provide a meaningful foundation to the organization—a foundation capable of supporting a structure and program which reflected the beliefs and priorities of the profession
>
> To determine priorities for action which reflected the desires and needs of the members of ALA, and to re-examine the organizational structure of ALA and all its committees, divisions, and round tables with the object of eliminating those units of the organization which were superfluous or irrelevant
>
> To create a structure that would involve a larger number of members in the programs and committee work of the organization.

The committee was to have the full cooperation of the ALA headquarters staff in its need for information to aid it in its search for a new direction for the association. Whenever, by a simple majority vote, the committee determined to do so, it should forward recommendations to any other ALA committee, round table, or division or to the Council or the Executive Board.

The subject of ALA's tax-exempt status comes up rather constantly now, and is thought by some to be a smoke screen behind which ALA hides when it does not want to undertake some particular activity. It came before the Council at the 1969 Annual Conference, and Council was asked to consider approving programs without regard as to whether the association's tax-exempt status might be forfeited. The problem here relates to the kind of tax exemption ALA enjoys. We are tax-exempt as an educational organization under the provisions of 501 (c) (3) in the U.S. Tax Code. As such a tax-exempt organization we may not engage in political matters, we must be circumspect in our relations with the Congress, and our programs and activities must reflect our educational status. The particular resolution on this subject was, wisely I think, not considered by the Council but was referred to an ad hoc committee for study.

At the 1970 Midwinter Meeting, the Junior Members Round Table presented suggestions to the Committee on New Directions for consideration. These included:

1. Limit personal membership in ALA to graduates of ALA-accredited library schools
2. Require continual professional education
3. Divisions to be headed by directors with authority to carry out policy established by divisional boards
4. Disband all divisions and form three new ones: Public Services, Technical Services, and Administrative Services
5. Trustees to become affiliated with ALA
6. Move headquarters to Washington.

The ALA Executive Board decided at this same meeting to open its meetings to observers from the membership of the association and the press, except for executive sessions where matters relating to the privacy of individuals and institutions are under discussion.

At the Midwinter Meeting in 1970, SRRT arranged for a resolution to be presented asking that the Council instruct the Committee on Program Evaluation and Support (COPES) to set aside enough money in the 1970–71 budget to cover some of the priorities recommended by the Committee on New Directions. The Executive Board acted on this and recommended the sum of $50,000 which was approved unanimously by Council.

Again, at the 1970 Midwinter Meeting, the Black Librarian's Caucus met and announced it would continue to meet at all ALA meetings to evaluate "progress being made by the Association in fulfilling its social and professional responsibilities to minority groups in the profession and in the nation." A resolution, developed by the caucus, dealing with library service to segregated institutions established to circumvent desegregation laws was presented to Council. This passed overwhelmingly by a roll-call vote (two negatives only), with the direction that it be sent to the governors of the states. As late as the Midwinter Meeting of 1971, there were no reports by the Black Caucus or other groups which provided further information on the subject of the resolution.

A resolution on recruitment from the membership meeting in Atlantic City in 1969 was put before the Council at the 1970 Midwinter Meeting. This asked that ALA re-examine and revitalize its recruitment policies for the profession, particularly in regard to minority groups and to our most promising young people. The resolution was referred to the Committee on New Directions without prejudice.

The 1970 Midwinter Meeting seemed to this observer to offer considerable promise. The young, impatient voices that began to be heard in 1968 were beginning to achieve results. They had created the Social Responsibilities of Libraries Round Table which appeared to be filling a need. Librarianship was ready, it seemed at that Midwinter, "to push itself out of its nest and fly off seeking its own." The editor of *American Libraries* wrote, "After Atlantic City in '69 and Midwinter '70 we are out of that nest and we are not going to be able to get back in."[8] Were we caught "in a whirlpool of dissension or . . . in the vortex of a new consensus?"

In the spring of 1970 the round table sent a letter on ALA letterhead containing a position statement on Cambodia and Southeast Asia to President Nixon and Senators Church and Cooper. This action by SRRT brings out a general difficulty about round tables—they are denied authority (under the Constitution and Bylaws of ALA) to make policy statements. In effect, SRRT did make a policy statement in its 1970 letter, and I'm sure that the recipients of the letter must have felt they had a position statement from the American Library Association, when in truth all they had was a statement from an affiliate of SRRT which had no authority to speak for and on behalf of ALA. Since ALA had taken no action which justified the letter, the Executive Board required SRRT to send another letter stating that the round table spoke without the approval of ALA. They were asked also to notify their affiliates that the affiliates could not take action in the name of ALA. I hope, but I do not know, that SRRT carried out all this request from the Executive Board.

Let me jump ahead to the spring of 1971. Again, SRRT took policy action. This time a member of SRRT sent a personal check to the Angela Davis defense fund indicating that the funds came from ALA and SRRT. SRRT then asked that the member be reimbursed by ALA. The answer to the round table had to be "No." Such a contribution was, it seemed, a statement of policy which was outside the authority of the round table. The round table resisted this instruction and will send a member to the 28–30 April 1971 meeting of the Executive Board to appeal the decision.[9]

In our chronology of events, we now move forward to the Annual Conference of 1970, and I want to present one occurrence and the subsequent actions by the Association. A section of the report of ACONDA dealing with intellectual freedom was under consideration at the membership meeting. An amendment, which would have provided funds as a "means to help meet the cost of living . . . for persons discharged or forced to resign" (in connection with intellectual freedom troubles) was defeated. At this time, the members of SRRT were invited by one of their members to stage a walkout "to show we will not stay in this type of Association." Approximately 100 left, but it was my observation that several returned after a few moments.

Let me now deal with subsequent actions that will show the association's present handling of complaints from librarians who claim they have been unjustly treated over issues of intellectual freedom, tenure, employment practices, and academic status. Council, at the 1969 Annual Conference, approved a program of action presented by the Intellectual Freedom Committee to help that committee and the Office for Intellectual Freedom deal with unjust treatment in the area of intellectual freedom. The Council meeting, at the same Annual Conference, considered a resolution from the Association of College and Research Libraries which proposed that ALA "adopt as official policy, the support of standards for all academic libraries by any and all appropriate professional means, including: (1) censure and sanctions, (2) accreditation of libraries." The standards referred to included rank, salary, sabbatical and other leaves, tenure, etc. The ALA Executive Board, in its study of the resolution, found the language ambiguous and could not recommend it to the Council for adoption. The resolution failed by a vote of 72 to 13. The president of ACRL announced, after the vote, that ACRL would proceed to "implement the standards as an ACRL action independent of ALA."

Complaints and requests for investigations in these several areas have continued to come to ALA headquarters in increasing numbers. There have been so many requests that a membership committee to deal with them expeditiously and fully was proposed by the president of the Library Administration Division. This was considered by the ALA Executive Board at its 1970 fall meeting, and a substitute proposal was approved under which a headquarters staff committee, composed largely of representatives of the ALA units involved, was established. This staff committee began meeting on 22 December 1970 and has met weekly since that time. At the 1971 Midwinter Meeting, there was a proposal that the association set up a "central mechanism" for the handling of investigations. A meeting was called of the concerned units of ALA which decided that, for the time being at least, the staff committee should act as this "central mechanism." This, of course, has to be approved by the Council of ALA and will be presented to the Council at the Annual Conference in Dallas this coming June. Staff should also be provided to assist the committee.

I have already referred to the establishment of ACONDA following the Annual Conference of 1969. The committee was appointed and set to work at once. The membership has remained intact except that the chairman, Frederick H. Wagman, became ill and was succeeded by Katherine Laich, and Mr. Richard Moses, appointed in August 1970, resigned after one session with the committee.

You have, perhaps, read the committee's reports. Perhaps you have heard them presented at a membership or a Council meeting. Let me, as briefly as I can, tell you of the committee's conclusions and the fate of its recommendations before the membership and Council. The first three recommendations of the committee were accepted by the association at the 1970 Annual Conference. These were:

1. (That) The American Library Association continue to be an organization for both librarians and libraries, with the overarching objective of promoting and improving library service and librarianship.

Note: This is an important objective. There had been much discussion to the point that ALA should become an organization for librarians *only*; there was, in fact, much discussion that ALA become a professional organization as distinct from its present status as an educational organization.

2. (That) The Association's highest current priorities be recognized and officially established as: Social Responsibilities; Manpower; Intellectual Freedom; Legislation; Planning, Research and Development; [and] Democratization and Reorganization.
3. (That) Substantially increased amounts of the Association's budget be directed toward implementation of these priorities.

ACONDA then proceeded to recommend specific action to be taken in each of the approved priority areas.

For social responsibilities, Council approved the recommendation that ALA

> define the broad social responsibilities of ALA in terms of (a) contribution that librarianship can make in ameliorating or even solving the critical problems of society, (b) support for all efforts to help inform and educate the people of the United States on these problems and to encourage them to examine the many views on, and the facts regarding, each problem, and (c) the willingness of ALA to take a position on current critical issues with the relationship to libraries and library service clearly set forth in the position statement.

Again in social responsibilities, the Council approved the recommendation that the association

> establish an ALA Office for Library Service to the Disadvantaged and the Unserved.

Note: There is as yet no budget for this office.

Further, the Council approved the recommendation that ALA

4. Expand the staff and budget of the Intellectual Freedom Office to enable it to engage in a nationwide informational program opposing censorship and in support of intellectual freedom, to conduct workshops for state and regional associations, and to help libraries develop educational programs.

Also, in the area of intellectual freedom, Council approved a proposal that the association

> make close and careful evaluation of the ability of the Freedom to Read Foundation to fulfill the expressed need of ALA for a means of providing grants to help meet the cost of legal action and, on an interim basis, the cost of living for individuals discharged or forced to resign because of their defense of intellectual freedom or in violation of their personal rights of freedom of expression or action; and if, within a reasonable time, the Foundation proves unable to reach a satisfactory level of performance, and further, if there is evidence to indicate that performance would be improved by bringing the functions of the Foundation within the Association, then action should be taken to that end; and that the Council requests a report at each annual and midwinter conference from the Freedom to Read Foundation.

Upon the recommendation of ACONDA, Council then voted that ALA

5. Enforce the existing policy which states that any member of the Association may serve simultaneously on not more than three committees or on one governing board/committee, excluding Council, and on two committees.

These actions, taken by Council, left a considerable number of matters in the ACONDA report without action, particularly those relating to democratization and reorganization.

At the Council meeting during the 1970 Annual Conference it was

> VOTED, That those items in the ACONDA Report not discussed and acted upon by Membership and/or Council be submitted to a

special ad hoc committee of Council to be named by the President for a report to be presented to Council at Midwinter 1971.

Council decided, further, that it would take action on the complete ACONDA report no later than the Dallas Annual Conference in 1971.

There was, of course, a membership meeting at the 1970 Annual Conference. Several items were added by SRRT or by individuals to the agenda of the meeting. These included:

1. A resolution on equal opportunities for women in librarianship, presented by the SRRT Task Force on Women's Liberation
2. A Librarian's Bill of Rights and a Statement on Proposed Ethics presented by SRRT
3. A resolution to hold future membership meetings at the beginning of the conference, preferably on the first day
4. A resolution from an Executive Board member deploring the destruction of libraries, library collections, and property and any disruption of the educational process resulting from such acts
5. A resolution to open all meetings of ALA to all members with the exception of meetings concerned with personal matters.

We come now, in the association's consideration of change, to the 1971 Midwinter Meeting in Los Angeles. The membership meeting in Los Angeles took up proposals that had been put on the agenda by previous meetings as well as new proposals. These included the following, with action taken as noted:

1. A motion to hold the membership meeting early in the week of midwinter FAILED.
2. The resolution on nondestruction of libraries CARRIED at the membership meeting and was later APPROVED by Council.
3. The motion to open all meetings to observers CARRIED at the membership meeting and was later APPROVED by Council with these words:

    THAT it be established policy of the ALA that all meetings of the Association be declared open to all members with closed meetings only for discussion of matters affecting the privacy of individuals or institutions.

4. The resolution to hold midwinter meetings outside of Chicago was amended to strike out reference to Chicago, leaving the sense of this resolution that ALA meet at midwinter in a climate

more temperate than that of Chicago, and then the resolution FAILED.
5. Resolutions relating to a Librarian's Bill of Rights and a Statement on Professional Ethics were referred by membership to the ALA Committee on Ethics.
6. A resolution calling for equal opportunity for women in librarianship was amended by membership to include a membership meeting on sex equality at the Dallas Annual Conference. This amendment FAILED, and the original motion CARRIED and was later APPROVED by Council with only a slight amendment.
7. A residency requirement for employment was presented. A suggestion that it be postponed until court decisions became clearer was made and DEFEATED. After various amendments it was CARRIED by membership and later by Council as follows:

> WHEREAS, it is the practice of numerous municipalities and other units of government to impose a requirement of local residency or U.S. Citizenship as a prerequisite for employment, and
> WHEREAS, these prerequisites have nothing to do with proper qualifications for library employment, such as ability, experience, etc., and
> WHEREAS, such rulings and practices can only aggravate the problem of obtaining qualified librarians, particularly in areas of lesser population or in relatively isolated locations,
> THEREFORE, The American Library Association is opposed to any rule, regulation, or practice imposing as a condition of new or continued employment in any library a requirement of residency or U.S. Citizenship, except where a demonstrable danger to national security is involved.

8. A resolution on fair representation on library boards was introduced and CARRIED at the membership meeting and was later APPROVED by Council. This reads:

> WHEREAS, the right to fair representation at the policy legislative level is the inherent right of those served by public facilities,
> WHEREAS, there is now no consistent policy to insure said representation,
> BE IT HEREBY RESOLVED, that the American Library Association vigorously support fair geographic and socio-economic representation of the total public served in the composition of all library governing boards, and

FURTHER, that the ALA responsibly communicate its position to all known officials empowered to make appointments to library governing boards.

No action was taken on another resolution from SRRT read into the record of the membership meeting. This concerned the American Indian, and the motion called upon ANACONDA to recognize the culture and values of the American Indian to the white majority, the need for library service to the American Indian, and also the recruitment to librarianship of American Indians.

Council, at the Los Angeles Midwinter Meeting, took additional action. It adopted: (1) a resolution on racial and sexual parity in library staffing, and (2) a resolution on compliance with fair employment practices.

Finally, the 1971 Midwinter Meeting turned to consideration of the ACONDA and ANACONDA reports. At the membership meeting a resolution "that the ALA staff develop and carry out the communications program [which ACONDA had developed in its study]" was approved. The membership meeting also considered a second recommendation from ACONDA. This called for "the development by ACONDA, using criteria developed by ACONDA, of a project under which skilled consultants" would study reorganization. ACONDA had, by this time, concluded that reorganization was beyond its efforts. After various motions, including one that the ACONDA members be the "skilled consultants," the recommendation passed the membership.

The membership meeting then moved to ACONDA's third recommendation which read:

> That, meanwhile [until the study by the skilled consultants is completed] Council accept the proposed changes in composition of Council and in procedures for nomination and election of Councilors, and request the Committee on Constitution and By-laws to prepare the necessary amendments to implement those changes.

The proposals affecting Council included these points:

1. The number of councilors should be 100, all elected at large, with 25 each year for a term of four years.
2. All councilors should be elected from within approximately ten geographic groupings of states, called districts.
3. All candidates for Council should be nominated by the ALA Nominating Committee or by membership petition.

4. A councilor elected to the Executive Board should be replaced for the remainder of his unexpired Council term at the next election by a new councilor from the same district.

The recommendation from ACONDA was amended to provide that until the management study was completed, the Council be constituted as follows:

100 Councilors elected at large and in addition one Councilor to represent each state and to be elected by the ALA members of each Chapter.

The amended motion CARRIED.

A final motion from ACONDA was passed at the membership meeting:

That, pending further study, decision, and action regarding reorganization of the Association, all divisions and sections of ALA examine rigorously the need for present permanent committees, and continue to maintain as permanent committees only those that are *essential* for continuing operation. The practice of appointing ad hoc committees or individual members to accomplish specific objectives should be followed whenever possible.

However, it was a different story when these recommendations reached the floor of the Council. All the recommendations considered by the membership at its January 1971 Midwinter Meeting were postponed by Council for further consideration at the Dallas Annual Conference in the summer of 1971.

A little while ago, I referred to Council's creation of a special ad hoc committee to make recommendations to it on matters in the ACONDA report not considered or discussed by membership and/or Council. This committee came to be known as ANACONDA, which is not an acronym. It really means a large snake which coils itself around its prey and crushes it. ANACONDA came to the 1971 Midwinter Meeting with recommendations in the areas of manpower; legislation; planning, research, and development; and democratization and reorganization.

ANACONDA's recommendation on manpower was amended at the membership meeting so that it read:

Combine ALA's existing staff activities relating to (1) library education and training, (2) recruitment, and (3) personnel utilization and concerns (including but not limited to salaries, status, welfare, employment practices, job definition, organization of personnel administration, tenure and ethics) into a new Office for Library Manpower to be responsible for the development of (1) appropriate programs, (2) standards and policies, and (3) procedures for the implementation of standards, e.g., investigations, mediation, sanctions.

The new Office for Library Manpower shall immediately undertake action to secure equality of opportunity in all aspects of manpower activities. It is intended that "equality of opportunity" will mean support for ALA programs designed to eliminate inequities on the basis of sex in library employment, and effective recruitment of men and women of ethnic and racial minorities to careers in the library profession.

After much discussion this recommendation was also deferred for further consideration to the Dallas Annual Conference.

ANACONDA had, for the 1971 Midwinter Meeting, three additional proposals. On the first of these three—legislation—it proposed that the budget and staff of the Washington office of ALA and the Committee on Legislation be strengthened; on planning, research, and development it recommended the establishment of a permanent Committee on Planning. These two proposals passed the membership meeting and the Council. On democratization and reorganization, ANACONDA supported the recommendation of ACONDA for a study by "skilled consultants" and suggested, further, that the presidents of chapters, divisions, and affiliates of ALA and chairmen of ALA committees be made an ex officio body of Council without vote.

Now, if all this has been clear enough for you to understand the course of study and conclusions since the Annual Conference of 1968, let me now try to indicate where we stand today and to suggest an evaluation of all these efforts.

First, as to where we stand. On the principal points, ACONDA must present at Dallas its proposal for a study of the organization of ALA by "skilled consultants." The committee now proposes, as a first option, that this study be headed by the new executive director whose appointment is hoped for by January of 1972; failing that, ACONDA would use library consultants. Second, the whole problem of the composition of Council must be considered. Third, the proposal for an Office for Library Manpower must also be considered at Dallas.

I am, of course, treading on unsure ground when I attempt an evaluation of what has happened since the Kansas City Annual Conference in 1968. Let me try, however, to touch upon the principal efforts since ALA began in 1968 to seek new directions.

The study of the Southwestern Library Association may result in more effective state and regional associations and more useful cooperation with ALA. The Activities Committee on New Directions for ALA has established the overriding objective and the top priorities of ALA and has encouraged proper financing of the priorities. The committee's work and its reports have caused the units of ALA, including chapters, to do a similar soul-searching.

The Round Table on the Social Responsibilities of Libraries has brought about serious consideration and analysis of several important aspects of librarianship and of the association. One may deplore, as I do, their methods, but the round table did shock ALA out of its sometimes glacial pace and it shook a considerable number of members out of their complacency. The Black Librarian's Caucus is serving well as the conscience of ALA in racial matters.

Meetings have been thrown open to all members, the ballots will be accompanied by statements of the candidates' professional concerns, the never ending fight against censorship has made new and important efforts, discussion is more free and full at Council and membership meetings, the association is providing thoughtful action where the rights of librarians are threatened, and the efforts at reorganization seek more meaningful involvement of the members. Read the resolutions passed by the association since 1968 and study them, and you will, I think, conclude that *much* change is going on in ALA.

Editor's Note: During the afternoon seminar, questions and discussion emphasized several significant points amplifying and expanding Mr. Clift's paper. Points of view reported here do not necessarily reflect Mr. Clift's opinions only, but also the opinions of faculty, students, and guests participating in the seminar.

Of primary interest were questions concerning the certification of librarians and the accreditation of libraries. The general consensus concerning certification of librarians was that this function was the responsibility of the individual states. Certification of librarians was encouraged, but it should be accomplished through the leadership of the State Library Extension Agency in accordance with standards established by that agency and endorsed by the state library association. It was suggested that in some situations a regulatory board should be created similar to boards established to certify medical and other professional groups. In other situations, certification of librarians might be combined with teacher certification, since both professions deal with educational processes and qualifications are primarily based on formal educational achievement.

The concept of accrediting libraries was also strongly endorsed. However, it was believed that the accrediting agent should be a national agency, namely, the American Library Association. Recognizing that standards of accreditation could be concerned with such matters as personnel administration, financial support, quality of service, and intellectual freedom, the participants felt that the greatest impact of accreditation would occur through a national program.

When questions concerning the future organization of the American Library Association arose, several points of view were expressed. The extensive proliferation of associations—local, state, regional, and national—was regretted by all. But perhaps library strength and unity could be improved if ALA became an umbrella organization or federation of autonomous associations. That each of the existing associations presently part of ALA (Public Library Association, for example) might even become autonomous was considered. These autonomous associations, coordinating functions, activities, and political strategy through federation with ALA, could then take a strong stance on national library policy.

Under the present organizational pattern, regional and state associations were urged to exercise a stronger voice in ALA matters. This could be accomplished by a more careful study of ALA issues by chapter membership and by chapter representatives to the ALA Council receiving more specific instruction from the state and regional association membership on positions to be taken.

Notes

[1] Accounts of the activities committees can be found in the *ALA Bulletin*. For a brief account of these committees prior to the present Activities Committee on New Directions for ALA, see Donald G. Davis, Jr., *The American Medical Association and the American Library Association* (Urbana, Ill., 1969). 60 leaves. Typewritten.
[2] *ALA Bulletin* 49:408–64 (Sept. 1955).
[3] *ALA Organizational Information, 1970–71* (Chicago: ALA). 152p.
[4] The membership voted in 1957 and 1967.
[5] Francis Bacon, *Maxims of the Law,* Preface.
[6] *ALA Bulletin* 62:819 (July-Aug. 1968).
[7] Ibid.
[8] *American Libraries* 1:235 (March 1970).
[9] The ALA Executive Board instructed that ALA reimburse the member.

LLOID B. JONES

THE *Educational* ENVIRONMENT

Every occupation has its own collection of trade stories, and education, thanks to the delightful vagaries of the young, has an abundant supply of anecdotes teachers love to tell. One of my favorites has to do with a fifth-grade class which was assigned to write an original composition. Each pupil might choose his own subject, but then whatever he wrote was to be strictly on that subject. The pupils were to be graded on their ability to stick to the subject. Little Mary, never one to take chances, chose as her subject, "The Universe, and Other Things." As I began to contemplate the subject of the changing educational environment of libraries, I remembered little Mary.

Consider the dimensions of the educational enterprise in America. During this academic year, there are more than 116,000 schools and colleges operating in the United States. They are attended by nearly 59 million students, and they employ more than 3 million teaching personnel. About 125,000 directors (trustees or board members) set out the policies which govern the decisions of a quarter of a million school and college administrators—management types who are this year spending some $70 billion.[1] At the same time, I discover, there are 24,000 libraries in the United States—lacking two—half of them public libraries and branches thereof, the rest institutional, special, professional, and so on.[2]

What are the relationships between these two vast systems, the effects upon libraries of their educational environment? Why, they, too,

---

Mr. Jones is coordinator of student laboratory experiences and professional certification in the School of Education, University of Denver. Before coming to the university, he served the Denver public schools in such capacities as director of curriculum, executive director of elementary education, etc.

are so numerous, so complex, so interwoven, as to be practically incomprehensible.

The people who use a given library, and who support that library, are first of all people who read. Their reading abilities, reading habits, and reading attitudes are determined by the effectiveness of the educational system from which they come, for the most part. The kinds of library services and materials those people want are a reflection of their level of learning, again a result of their educational experiences. The same must be said of their habits of inquiry, the ways they seek to find out what they want to know. So, also, are determined their tastes in recreation and in cultural pursuits. The scope of their interests derives basically from the same source—education—whether it be narrow or wide.

Thus one can with only superficial analysis identify five ways in which the educational environment bears upon the library, and those five are in turn so interdependent that one must reckon the relationships as five factorial, or 120, as a conservative estimate. The 120 must be multiplied by the 24,000 libraries and then by the 116,000 elementary schools, junior and senior high schools, and colleges—public, parochial, and independent—in this country.

Now you can appreciate my sense of shock as I recognized the galactic dimensions of the subject I had agreed to discuss—the universe, and other things. You will also, I trust, understand the derivation of my thesis, which is that people in library work have a vital concern with what is going on in education, and they must in their own interest not merely inform themselves but also vigorously participate in shaping the course of educational events. From that position, let us take a look at some few aspects of the current educational environment, recognizing that any such survey must necessarily be limited, selective, and suggestive rather than either comprehensive or definitive.

Any discourse on environment in these days must, it appears, deal with three topics: pollution, mutation, and depletion. So that we may be in step with the times, let us analyze the educational environment for pollution, mutation, and depletion.

Human beings have to breathe, and when the substance they breathe consists of not only air but also noxious materials, we call the phenomenon "pollution." The learning functions of the human organism—thinking, feeling, behaving, becoming—are almost equally instinctive, nearly as sure to be carried on to some extent even without a conscious exercise of will.

The substance taken in through these learning processes comes from, among other sources, books. In this meeting I would suppose I would get no argument on that point. Now go to the nearest bookstall or newsstand or even to the airport. Scan the titles and the cover blurbs of the books offered for sale. Adult books, they're called. What you find, I submit, is material which obviously is conducive to intellectual and moral and spiritual emphysema—educational pollution.

Everyone here is aware of other pollutants in the educational atmosphere: fallout, so to speak, carried by television, radio, motion pictures, newspapers and other periodicals, the games people play, the diversions we seek, the advertising we heed—we of the Pepsi generation.

You have sensed, no doubt, my tacit assumption that learning is the measure of education. We learn that to which we give attention. Our attention is claimed, in this day and age, by much that is at best trivial and at worst debasing. In these times, the atmosphere of education is saturated with gunk. Pollution.

And what of mutation, the occurrence of life forms so strange as to be unrecognizable? Mutant forms appear in environments where unaccustomed conditions or new stresses come to bear on ordinary creatures. Thus, the camel, a horse put together by a committee. Thus such educational paradoxes as the street academy, the free university, the halfway house, the nonschool (for nonlearners).

Let us create for viewing a hypothetical prototype and name it, in the contemporary fashion, YOTE—Youth Opposed to Education. YOTE's objective is to teach its enrollees only to endure, to tolerate themselves and one another. The content of YOTE's curriculum is trauma, the bitter memories of neglect and abuse and defeat each member has experienced. YOTE's basic procedure is the rap session, the emotionally charged exchange of life stories in the most intimate and devastating detail. To pass examinations at YOTE, one must be able to cry out in anguish, "Heebie, I love you! Will you love me, Heebie?" If you and Heebie fall spontaneously into each other's arms, you get a grade A.

In all solemnity I assure you the foregoing is neither exaggeration nor caricature. Neither, of course, is it a description of all enterprises adjunct to the system of conventional schools and colleges. Let there be no question that YOTE and all its variants are admirable humane enterprises, doing enormous good for rejects from our societal assembly line.

But can this be education? Well, every YOTE I know of draws its funds, its facilities, and its staff from sources which would otherwise be available to conventional forms of education. But then the duck-billed platypus, viewed from a certain angle, no doubt resembles a duck. Every observer can cite his own instances, some of them phenomena occurring within established schools and colleges. They could, of course, be harbingers of the future. From here, the whole mélange looks more like educational mutation.

The educational environment also is showing signs of depletion, ominous signs that we are using up irreplaceable resources and rapidly nearing the end of available supply. The figure, applied to the process of education, has to do not with material but with human resources, and perhaps there is no such thing as an irreplaceable human resource. Or is there?

A sizable group of people have come out of our schools and colleges —often our "best" schools and colleges—with . . . nothing. They have beat a philosophical retreat back across nine hundred years to take up a position beside another protestor of another land and another language. Translated from the Persian or translated from the "Mod," the message is still the same:

A Book of Verses underneath the Bough,
A Jug of Wine, a Loaf of Bread—and Thou
Beside me singing in the Wilderness—
Oh, Wilderness were Paradise enow!

One is tempted to substitute for the word "jug" the word "pot." One is tempted to advise these escapists that this much-abused planet no longer has any wildernesses, only some areas where we try to restrict the use of tote-goats. But levity is not in order.

The fact is that, for these persons, our educational system has contributed nothing either to their peace of mind as individuals or to their capability for promoting the general welfare and securing the blessings of liberty to ourselves and our posterity. One cannot help thinking of a parallel system which has developed the capability of producing 10 million automobiles a year, only to find the world supply of petroleum perilously near the point of exhaustion. There are plenty of informed observers who declare that the educational system likewise is running out of gas.

No less an authority than John Fischer, president of Teachers College, Columbia, writing for the prestigious *Saturday Review,* asks bitterly, "Who Needs Schools?"[3] In the same issue of the same magazine, Peter Schrag takes as his title, "End of the Impossible Dream."

Schrag defines the impossible dream: "that the schools constitute the ultimate promise of equality and opportunity; that they enable American society to remain somehow immune from the economic inequities and social afflictions that plague the rest of mankind; that they, in short, guarantee an open society."[4]

If that is not truly a description of an impossible dream, it will have to do until a better comes along. All the Congress said in the Ordinance of 1787 was that, enlightenment and understanding being necessary to free people, schools and the means of education should be forever preserved.

Yet it has become highly popular, in both publication and public discussion, to "bad-mouth" education. Representative is a statement by Charles Silberman in the report of a three-year study of teacher education financed by the Carnegie Corporation:

> Because adults take the schools for granted, they fail to appreciate what grim, joyless places most American schools are, how oppressive and petty are the rules by which they are governed, how intellectually sterile and esthetically barren the atmosphere, what an appalling lack of civility obtains on the part of teachers and principals, what contempt they unconsciously display for children as children.[5]

One whose daily duties have for two decades included visiting schools, many schools, finds it hard to reconcile that description with what he sees—and hears, and feels. It is a view which is also difficult to relate to Americans' long-standing and general concern about dropouts. If schools and colleges are like that, the best thing we could do for students is to get them out of school and keep them out.

But here is an opinion widely shared. In this environmental study of education I have chosen to call this debility of the spirit "educational depletion." If, as sometimes appears, our human resources of courage, energy, and anticipation of good are permanently deplenished, we are truly in a bad way.

To recapitulate, I am saying that the changing educational environment of libraries is characterized, as is the physical environment in these times, by pollution, mutation, and depletion. There follows, then, the question of what is to be done. Let us assume most of us are not ready to seek the quickest and least painful method of suicide without first considering possible alternatives.

The answer to the question is coming at us from every direction. The answer is, in a word, "Innovate!" Social scientists say, "Education must innovate." Technologists say, "Education must innovate." Candidates for the school board say, "The schools must innovate."

Consequently, schools and colleges are innovating like crazy. The educational environment of libraries is aswarm with educational innovations. If you do not yet have on your racks and your bound-volume shelves a journal called "Educational Innovations," all I can say is, Yankee opportunism ain't what it used to be.

But innovation, I submit, is a good thing, or it could be a good thing. Out of the feverish search for new ideas might come the refutation of the Fischers and the Schrags and the Silbermans. In all this frenzied experimentation lies a substantial hope that the educational environment will restore itself to a state of wholesomeness, and wholesome within a set of largely new conditions.

Yes, the educational scene is swarming with changes: some of them significant, I expect, some of them inconsequential, some transitory, some portending a new era. If anyone would try to tell you which is which, I would admire his daring and damn his judgment. As well as to have asked a carriage maker in the year 1901 to conceive the year 1971 and predict which of the contraptions then being worked on by Benz and Daimler and Olds and Winton and Ford and Maxwell and Stanley would become the commonly used vehicle of the future.

I can, however, identify four fundamental, environment-altering structural shifts which are occurring in the educational landscape. They are, I think, neither temporary nor superficial, but rather are long, slow-moving trends. One can learn of their beginnings years ago; one can anticipate their continuing for years to come. To be sure, there are momentary flurries of a sort of volcanic activity, and there are periodic reversals. But in the long view, these movements appear to be steady, and sure, and very basic.

The first of these changes in the depths of education is individuation. By the term *individuation* I refer to a "process by which social individuals become differentiated one from the other; [forming] into a separate and distinct entity."[6]

This is no new trend. It has been known for a long time that every human being is in certain essential respects different from any other human being who ever lived, and that individuality is infinitely precious. You may date this concept back to Alfred Binet and the measurement of abilities. You may credit the concept to Gregor Mendel and his laws of heredity. You may attribute the ultimate truth of it to Jesus of Nazareth. In any case it is not new. But with the enormous growth of population, and the parallel growing menace of anonymity, realization of one's individuality has come to be of ultimate importance. Education is adjusting its practices to bring forth that uniqueness of the person.

Right now you can read reams about individualized instruction. A while back there was the ungraded school, CAI (Computer-Assisted Instruction), IGE (Individually Guided Education), and on and on and on. Some one or more of all these current manifestations may be profoundly significant. It is that question which we cannot answer. What we can say, I submit, is that one day the educational environment will be so constituted as to foster the discovery and development of the distinguishing quality of every individual in it.

Schools and colleges are immeasurably closer to that goal than they were twenty or fifty or seventy-one years ago. Progress is constantly impeded by unease about standards and by our American obsession with statistics. Yet slowly but surely, by one means or another, education is consciously moving toward discovering the unique characteristics of every individual, determining objectives peculiarly appropriate for him, devising a particular set of strategies, a program, to enable him to reach those objectives, and measuring his progress with his individual yardstick. The result—and again this is a relative rather than an absolute observation—is individuality identified and realized. From another viewpoint the result is individualism rampant—on a field of crimson.

We see elementary schoolchildren walking around and around their school carrying signs in a picket line. We see junior high school pupils sitting down in the main hall and refusing to go to class until the principal has given them assurance that things will be changed to their liking. We see senior high youth rioting, just among themselves and then taking on the faculty and the police, closing down the institution. We see college students taking possession of a section of campus, setting up a kind of military encampment which eventually has to be removed by military force. These are products of the individualized American educational system.

For years, in the American classroom, one has seldom heard the statement, "That's right," or "That's wrong," or even—leaving the moral connotation out of it—"That's correct or incorrect." Rather, it's, "What do you think?" "Do you agree?" "State it in your own words," "Have you any questions?" Such has been the atmosphere of American education for decades, so that it has influenced the attitudes not only of today's students but of their parents and grandparents. We have deliberately and with increasing emphasis fostered individualism by such unobvious means as well as by such obvious measures as the elective system and so on down to today's individualized instruction. The effort has been consummately effective—to some people appallingly effective.

Yet is not the present turmoil simply a phase—squalls, so to speak, along the path of the Gulf Stream? I think so. I think in due time we will come to another phase in which the expressions of individuality will be conservative rather than obstructive and productive rather than merely noisy. That phase will occur as and when we discover what such constructive and productive forms of individual expression can be, and teach them in the schools and colleges. Nevertheless, if one can see past the turmoil of the moment, it is evident that individuation is an emerging characteristic of the changing educational environment.

A second truly fundamental shift in education is the recognition and cultivation of varied styles of learning, all of them entirely respectable. To understand what is occurring here, it is necessary to keep in mind that learning is both a product and a process. Time was when Learning, the product, usually spelled with a capital L, was generally considered to be synonymous with information, and the information was expressed either in words or in the symbols of mathematics and science.

Educators knew, of course, that there were also skills, attitudes, concepts, appreciations, ideals, and so on, but somehow these tended to remain peripheral. Probably Benjamin Bloom was the individual who did most to "get it all together" when he established the legitimacy of the Affective Domain and the Psycho-Motor Domain along with the Cognitive Domain.[7]

As Bloom's *Taxonomy* has been more and more widely studied and understood, there has been increasing acceptance of the idea that Learning, the product, does indeed include skills and attitudes and appreciations and so on as core elements along with knowledge. With this acceptance is coming—slowly—realization that learning, the process, consists of more than reading, reciting, and writing words and numbers. For example, one doesn't learn to respond to the *1812 Overture* or to paint a landscape or to play golf by reading a book or by talking about the matter, although, to be sure, those procedures are sometimes tried, especially in the locker room at the end of a round of golf.

With recognition that different learning objectives require different learning activities has come the understanding that different persons learn best in different ways. Here is evident a close connection with the concept of individuation. Some people learn best by reading; others need to see, to view, in order to understand; some must feel, touch, manipulate; still others benefit most from physical activity, acting it out. And so on. In fact, it appears that every individual has a distinctive pattern or combination of learning activities which is most productive for him. This realization is gradually altering education practice.

I cite the instance of a third grade studying sentence structure by physical movement. Each of seven children represented a word which was lettered large on a cardboard rectangle he carried. The children arranged and rearranged themselves to form sentences—declarative, interrogative, and so forth—including some word combinations which, as they said, "wouldn't work." At other times these children studied the same subject by different means. Their classroom, incidentally, was not a grim and joyless place. Silberman must have missed it.

This whole subject of learning styles is a fascinating one, and it should not be dropped without at least a nod in the direction of Marshall McLuhan. Media are right now very big in education. In perspective, however, the judicious use of varied media in the teaching-learning situation seems to be not so much a separate development as an aspect of the major trend toward learning about learning.

A third massive transformation is occurring in the world-surface of education, manifesting itself in the appearance of new curricula. You can get a lively argument on this point, an argument with many sides. One side is that the so-called new curricula are not real. Some say they are just new names for long-established concepts; others contend that the only new element is a new approach, which they term the "interdisciplinary approach." I make no claims as a scholar, but there would seem to me to be an enormous distance between the seven liberal arts—grammar, logic, rhetoric, arithmetic, geometry, astronomy, music—and the program of a contemporary college of arts and sciences: ecology, urban studies, the black experience, mass communications, mental hygiene.

Such changes, to be sure, have occurred only over a period of several hundred years, by gradual stages. But that is exactly the point: in the course of time, new curricula have appeared, are appearing, and will continue to appear. Whether any of the new curricula now in vogue will survive is uncertain and hardly important. What is important is that they will survive if they meet the test of relevance.

The word "relevant" is being bandied about a great deal just now, and, like so many latter-day shibboleths, it represents an attempt to enunciate a principle which merits examination. Jerome Bruner approached the principle from one direction when he stated that any discipline can be presented to a learner of any age in ways that are understandable and meaningful to him.[8] The reciprocal statement is needed here: teachers and learners can find ways of organizing mankind's store of learning into disciplines—curricula—which are understandable and meaningful under conditions of life that now exist. That is what relevance is all about, and it is a major educational development because the educational system is beginning to recognize the right, even the obligation, of teachers and learners to seek constantly for new and more relevant curricula.

A fourth long-term, broad-scope trend I think I see in the educational environment is the emergence of the school-centered community. It would be more accurate to say re-emergence. In the largely rural America of the turn of the century, the place of a family's residence was commonly identified by its school. There, at the schoolhouse, the children were educated, the political parties caucused, the ice-cream socials and Saturday-night dances were held, and likewise the rare concert or play—any cultural event which might come to the countryside. In the community where I lived, religious services were held in the school on Sunday. The school was a place of belonging.

But, nearly two hundred years ago, Americans chose for themselves a way of life aimed toward affluence, and consequently it is interdependent, and therefore complex, and inevitably pluralistic. The direction was set without, of course, foreseeing the ultimate outcome. One outcome is that now I live somewhere in an urban sprawl, not a neighborhood, a vicinity. I can live there without anyone, almost, knowing me. Since almost no one knows me, I can easily conclude that no one cares about me. If no one cares about me, it matters little what I do, be it legal or illegal, ethical or unethical, moral or immoral, responsible or irresponsible. The urban sprawl has advantages and modern conveniences beyond the wildest dreams of our founding fathers, but one thing it doesn't have. It has no place of belonging.

Recently there have been moves, as in Flint, Michigan, to re-establish within American life—urbanized—places of belonging. In Flint it is an elementary school where once more the children are educated, but the building is also in use as much as sixteen hours a day, year round, for recreational, social, cultural, political activities. These are the surface phenomena. More deeply, here is a place of belonging, of knowing and being known, of expressing concern and loyalty and pride and responsibility. Here is the locus and focus of a community, as distinguished from an area or a district or a postal zone identified by a zip code. Here is a sign that the school will once more move into the center of American living as a vital and unifying force.

Let me immediately dispel the notion that the foregoing might be a subtle plug for the neighborhood school, which has been described as a northern euphemism for the ugly fact of segregated and discriminatory education. It has been demonstrated, in Berkeley, California, for instance, that, transportation being what it is today, community need not be confused with vicinity. It has been demonstrated also in Denver, Colorado. Among the schools I have personally worked with are several whose pupils come from three or four or five separate, widely separated, parts of the city. More significant, the pupils' parents and other relatives also come—to *their* school. The essential element in these school-centered communities is not geography; the vital factor is sense of community, common concern, and mutual support. In such developments, occurring without fanfare in many parts of the country, there is justification for faith that education in American life is not an obsolescent institution but a reviving and revitalizing force.

To recapitulate now a second time, I am saying there are trends in education which support the belief that the changing educational environment will become more invigorating, more wholesome, more vital to the American people than any of us now dares to imagine. Our first recapitulation a while ago suggested that the educational environment is rapidly approaching a state in which it can no longer support life, so to speak.

We have reasoned our way into a dichotomy, and, in my considered judgment, it is very real. The educational system could be heading toward virtual and relatively rapid dissolution, with concomitant very grave effects upon libraries. By George Orwell's famous target date of 1984, Big Brother would have little need of libraries. He would require only a few government archives, those carefully regulated and restricted in use to politically trustworthy governing officials. Hitler's Germany was not far off this course. It can happen.

On the opposite course, schools and colleges could become truly exhilarating, truly individuating, truly emancipating, truly humane institutions. Then libraries would move forward in a period of tremendous expansion and enormously increased usefulness. Then we could predict that much of the routine drudgery of library work, and schoolwork as well, could be turned over to computers. Then we could think of the Dewey Decimal System being replaced by a system in the language of FORTRAN (Formula Translating system) or ALGOL (Algorithmic Oriented Language), using binary rather than decimal numbers.

We could even speculate upon the storage and retrieval not merely of information but of aesthetic experiences, psychomotor skills, understandings, attitudes, appreciations. We can foresee libraries stocked extensively with nonprint materials in a wide variety of media.

Two completely different prospects, and the differences are crucial. So what are the probabilities? In which kind of educational environment can libraries be expected to live between now and the twenty-first century?

Environmental studies have, not uncommonly, a way of reaching a point where one is overwhelmed. Environmental conditions are so pervasive, so complex, so diffuse that one can comprehend them only in figurative terms. You can't grab smog. Environmental forces are so stupendous, so inexorable, so imperceptible in their movement that one who would hope to affect them feels he is tilting at a windmill.

In the instance of the educational environment of libraries, however, I contend that such frustrations are not inevitable. Education at this juncture is thoroughly shaken, unsettled, unfixed. As military men say, the situation is fluid. To put it another way, education is ripe for change. Also, education at this time is diffused; some would say fragmented. One school is not like another school; one college is very different from another college. The meaning of this situation, for our purposes here, is that education is broken up into its get-at-able parts.

In other words, right now it is still possible for a group of people to shape their particular sector of the educational environment the way they want it. If the people of just one of those 24,000 libraries and the people of the college or schools which make up that library's educational environment so will, they can to a considerable extent control their destiny. This, I repeat, is the central thesis of this discourse.

This proposition should not be accepted naively. There are limits. There are budgets. There are policies. There are attitudes. But budgets can be raised. Policies can be revised. Attitudes can be changed. Not without effort. Not without time. Not without more frequent, more regular, and more mutual communication than an occasional colloquium. Not, in short, without commitment.

No millennium is being hinted at, but much can be done. There is no reason a given school or college or subsystem of education in a given locality need be "grim and joyless, intellectually sterile, and esthetically barren." There is no reason a given library or library system need be impersonal, inaccessible, haughtily unconcerned, and devoted chiefly to bookkeeping. Not if the people in such an environmental subsystem really want it otherwise.

People in library work and people in education can, and in my opinion must, for the sake of their own survival, effectively join forces and move forward not merely to await the future but to shape the future. As I have said, conditions are likely never to be more favorable. We made the educational system and the library system of this country what they are today, did we not? Then there is no insurmountable reason we cannot take what we have made and transform it into what we want it to become.

Four hundred years ago my favorite author stated it well. "There is a tide in the affairs of men, which, taken at the flood, leads on to fortune."

Ladies and gentlemen, the tide is at the flood. Now.

NOTES

[1]Data taken from annual statistical reports of the U.S. Office of Education and the National Education Association, 1970.

[2]Eleanor F. Steiner-Prag and Helaine MacKeigan, compilers, *1970–71 American Library Directory* (New York: Bowker, 1970), p. vii.

[3]John H. Fischer, "Who Needs Schools?" *Saturday Review* 53:78 ff. (19 Sept. 1970).

⁴Ibid., p.68.

⁵Charles E. Silberman, *Crisis in the Classroom* (New York: Random, 1970), p.10.

⁶*The American Heritage Dictionary of the English Language* (New York: American Heritage, 1969), p.670–71.

⁷Benjamin S. Bloom, *The Taxonomy of Educational Objectives* (New York: Longmans, 1954).

⁸Jerome S. Bruner, *The Process of Education* (Cambridge, Mass.: Harvard University Press, 1960), p.47.

JOHN T. EASTLICK

THE *Librarian's* ENVIRONMENT

Many persons have tried to determine whether librarianship is truly a profession. The definitions of professionalism as evolved by other professional organizations have been carefully studied and compared to those of librarianship. One of the most perceptive studies of professionalism in librarianship was accomplished by Dale E. Shaffer.[1] He identified nineteen criteria for evaluating professionalism. Six of the criteria emphasize the educational base of professionalism—not only the basic "distinctive, systematic and defined body of highly specialized professional knowledge . . . " but also the continuing "programs of research." After a thorough analysis of Shaffer's criteria for professional status, Joan Harrigan synthesizes professionalism as follows:

> A profession requires a systematic, organized, distinctive and common body of knowledge, theory, skills and terminology, supported and constantly expanded by research. The means for achieving this intellectual tradition is professional education based on a broad, liberal and humanizing education. The structure which provides this education is the graduate school of librarianship. A profession also requires an organizational structure within which members of the profession can interact to provide mutual protection, exert control over action of its members, provide professional solidarity and maintain high standards of training and performance. The means for achieving these purposes are membership standards for admission and/or certification; standards for library education and for the operation of its institutions;

Mr. Eastlick served as Librarian of the Denver Public Library from 1951 to 1969. In 1969 he was appointed professor in librarianship, Graduate School of Librarianship, University of Denver.

statements of philosophy, ideals of service, and organizational purposes; and a Code of Ethics defining the individual's relationship to his clients, to his peers and to society. The professional individual is one who has experienced the educational background provided by the library school and who voluntarily accepts the rights and duties imposed on him by his professional organization.[2]

If we can accept Harrigan's synthesis, we then recognize that librarianship is moving toward full stature as a profession. But the years and decades ahead will have to be filled with action to solidify, to clarify, and to refine the status of professionalism. Earlier I used the term "the emerging profession." That, I believe, is where we are—well on the way, going the right direction, but with much yet to be done in research, in the clarification of the roles of the professional association, and in the establishment of criteria for individual admission to and continuance in the profession.

From the definition of professionalism it can clearly be seen that the basic elements include education, knowledge, and research. These elements are primarily the responsibility of the library schools. It is not the intent of this paper to review the history of library education. Suffice it to say that library education has moved in a short number of years from the apprenticeship and in-service library training, through the period of organized library training classes, to the period of the college- and university-affiliated library school, accompanied by the development of accreditation procedures. Some library educators believe that a fourth period has developed from the mid-1940s to the present, characterized as an era of experimental change in curriculum and degree structure.

It is to this "experimental" period that we need to address ourselves. Starting in the late 1940s, it has accelerated as we have proceeded through the 1960s and into the decade of the 1970s. For a period of time library education seemed to be blanketed in a traditionalism which prohibited library educators from recognizing new trends and new developments in library-related activities, programs, and functions. As a result we saw a tendency to splinter library education, with the media specialist going off in one direction and the information science specialist going off in another. It is unfortunate that these areas of library-related activities splintered away from the core discipline of librarianship. However, there is a trend now for these subject areas to become again related closely to the core field of librarianship. After all, the media specialist and the information scientist build their programs and develop their services on primary concepts of the field of librarianship. They utilize many of the same philosophies and techniques. Even though new hardware and new equipment make the processes different, the end product of the transference of knowledge and of the organization, storage, and retrieval of information still is the core and basic element of librarianship. All segments of the broad field of librarianship must unite around a common body of knowledge upon which the profession is founded.

It is not enough, however, merely to maintain a body of professional knowledge. The expansion of that professional knowledge must be rigorously pursued. Generally, librarians and library educators have tended to perform research dealing with items of minutiae. Only a few of the great minds in librarianship have tried to face and accomplish research of real social significance. Even when such research is accomplished, the practicing librarian has a tendency to ignore that research and fails to put its findings into practice.

The librarian of the future must be research-oriented. If the professional interest of the individual librarian prohibits the accomplishment of research, at least the individual must be capable of evaluating, interpreting, and applying research to library activities.

The achievement of a master's degree in librarianship from an accredited library school is not the end educational experience for the professional librarian today; it is only the beginning. As new technologies develop, as subject fields grow, and as the social environment of the library requires new programs and new activities, practicing librarians will find it essential not only to participate in short-time workshops and institutes but also to return to an academic institution to pursue advanced study which will bring them to that currency and relevancy essential to their job.

One should not discuss professionalism without mentioning the problem of the present overproduction of library school graduates. Other highly recognized and respected professions through their national associations limit the number of individuals who can enter training in any given year. Should the library profession do the same thing? Even though the present job shortage for librarians is credited to the current economic pressures of inflation and rising taxes, one cannot help but wonder whether this is the basic cause.

During the past few years several new library schools have been accredited by the ALA Committee on Accreditation. As of February 1971 there were forty-seven accredited library schools in the United States and six in Canada. Rumor has it that numerous other institutions are planning such schools and will request accreditation. Are all these existing and planned library schools really necessary?

It is possible that we can dilute or eradicate the value of the professional librarian by overproduction. Because the profession in past years has been primarily a female profession, a large attrition of available librarians has been anticipated because of marriage. But in this era of planned parenthood and limited families, will this attrition occur? With the introduction of the library technician and the library associate, will as many librarians performing truly professional functions be required? Although there always will be some attrition and not all graduates of accredited library schools will be utilized to their full professional capacity, the library profession as a whole should carefully consider the limiting of the number of accredited library schools and the size of enrollments.

Future librarians will find themselves working for a different kind of organization than they have worked for in the past. Librarians have operated in a hierarchical structure with power and authority flowing from the top position to the lower echelons of service. This bureaucratic form of organization has not been bad, though it has prohibited some staff members with unusual creativity and innovativeness from undertaking projects and activities outside normal routine duties. In many of the hierarchical organizations the quality of supervision given to the lower service levels has been weak and inconcise. This has resulted in staff members' not always knowing what their full duties were and how their duties related to other staff duties. Therefore, the staff member had little feeling of responsibility for the end product of the library.

Although it is apparent that the bureaucratic structure of administration is not going to be altered drastically, it is very probable that the future librarian will find a modification of this structure. Several recent events are changing the structure. Events are occurring that require the clarification of duties and the more specific assignment of responsibilities for all levels of employees. In recent years we have seen the introduction of the budgetary process known as Program, Planning, and Budgeting, which requires not only the definition of specific, measurable objectives but also the definition of programs by which those objectives are carried out. Each program must be evaluated in terms of cost versus the benefit received. Program, Planning, and Budgeting has evolved into other forms of personnel and budget management. Performance budgeting has recently been evolved by which standards of performance are quantitatively measured. All these new techniques and philosophies of management, though still couched in the hierarchical structure of organization, are transferring to the individual employee a greater degree of responsibility. Each employee in reality is becoming accountable for his actions and for the services he provides as a result of his employment. Leon Lessinger, former U.S. Office of Education Associate Commissioner for Elementary and Secondary Education, is the originator of the concept of accountability. Utilizing Lessinger's basic concepts but translating them into library philosophy, we may define library accountability as "the reporting to appropriate and/or official designees by the responsible agent of results achieved in terms of fiscal accounting for funds expended to achieve those results on a least cost/most benefit basis."[3] No longer will the library employee be able to slough off responsibility or to operate within a framework of ill-defined duties. Those responsibilities to which he has been assigned must be clear, definite, and measurable.

It is probable that in order to achieve accountability a new form of supervision of library personnel will evolve. No longer will short-term assignments be made to personnel of a library. Rather, long-term objectives will be outlined, discussed, and agreed upon by the supervisor and the worker. The worker will then proceed to fulfill those objectives. This represents the philosophy of management by objective. Such philosophy does not weaken the supervisor's power or position in the hierarchy, nor does it change the responsibility and accountability of the employee. But it gives the employee a greater freedom of utilizing innovativeness and creativeness in performing those tasks for which he is accountable. It will mean that the employee has greater potential for individual growth than that previously experienced by library employees. It also means that the employee will have to be more dedicated, knowledgeable, and service-oriented to carry out those objectives which he has been assigned.

No doubt other elements of the professional librarian's environment will change in the future. The length of the work week will shorten; the influence of the library union—be it school, academic, or public—will increase; fringe benefits as part of the conditions of employment will increase. But I believe strongly that the greatest changes of the future will occur in the areas already emphasized: (1) the evolution of a true profession based on a growing, dynamic knowledge base; (2) the emergence of a strong national professional association; and (3) the development of new patterns of administration which will at the same time make the professional librarian more accountable for the quality and quantity of his work while offering him the opportunity to be more innovative in the performance of his job.

NOTES

[1]Dale E. Shaffer, *The Maturity of Librarianship as a Profession* (Metuchen, N.J.: Scarecrow Press, 1968).

[2]Joan Harrigan, "Librarianship—A Profession?" (unpublished paper, Graduate School of Librarianship, University of Denver, 1971).

[3]Joan Harrigan, "Library Accountability" (unpublished paper, Graduate School of Librarianship, University of Denver, 1971).